Anonymous

Discovering the Somebody You Are to God

A Bible Study by

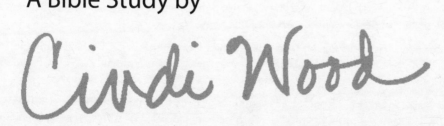

Nashville / Abingdon Press

Contents

About the Author

Cindi Wood is a sought-after speaker and Bible teacher and the author of the popular *Frazzled Female* series. Combining biblically-based teaching with humor from daily experience, she offers hope and encouragement to women of all ages and walks of life as she speaks to groups across the United States and internationally. Through her writing, conferences and events, and other engagements and interviews, Cindi's committed passion and practical delivery help women to discover joyful living through a deep encounter with Jesus Christ. In addition to the *Frazzled Female* books and Bible study, she is the author of *Desperate: Seeking Simplicity . . . Finding the Cross*; *Too Blessed for This Mess*; and *I've Used All My Sick Days, Now I'll Have to Call in Dead*. Cindi and her husband, Larry, live in Kings Mountain, North Carolina, and enjoy ministry partnership with their two adult sons and daughters-in-law.

Follow Cindi:

 @CindiWoodAuthor

 @CindiWoodMinistries

 @CindiWoodAuthor

Web   FrazzledFemale.com

(check here also for event dates and booking information)

Introduction
Your Personal Invitation with R.S.V.P.

Have you ever felt anonymous—overlooked, unimportant, or bruised by the world? We all have at one time or another. But there's good news. While the opinions of others may drag us down, the God who created us has an entirely different opinion of who we are. That's because we are His creations, and everything He created is good!

The women I encounter as I live and teach and speak are looking for ways to make a difference in their daily lives. Each of us—whether we're working women, stay-at-home moms, or women moving into our retirement years—wants to be a *somebody* who makes a positive impact in the world around us. *Anonymous: Discovering the Somebody You Are to God* is designed specifically to help you discover your uniqueness and significance to Christ!

The Invitation

When I was a middle-school teacher, a colorful invitation with R.S.V.P. hung on the door of my classroom to greet my sixth-grade students on the first day of school. Before they ever entered my classroom, I extended a friendly welcome, asking them to accept my invitation to a fun and challenging year ahead. Signing their names to the R.S.V.P. denoted their acceptance of my terms and declared them a bona-fide "Wood Wonderkid."

I'd like to extend to you, my friend, an invitation with an R.S.V.P.! And yes, I do want you to sign it and agree to the terms, because I know the high drop-out rate among busy women attending Bible studies. This invitation includes six weeks of fun and relevant study of four "anonymous" women of the Bible who were known and remembered not by their names but by their circumstances:

The Woman Who Anointed Jesus – *Judged*
The Woman with the Issue of Blood – *Hurting*
The Woman at the Well – *Ordinary*
The Woman Who Committed Adultery – *Shame*

Though we do not know their names, all of these women were known and loved by God. And when each woman encountered Jesus, she was never the same again!

As we consider each woman's story, including the cultural influences and lifestyles of her day, we will discover powerful ways that we all can relate to and learn from each of them. By digging into God's Word, we will mine our way to discover the jewels of God's mercy and grace.

By accepting this invitation to dig into the stories of these four women, you are agreeing to be faithful to come before the Lord in prayer and reflection as you make your way through this study. You also are committing to come before Him in agreement with His Word, hiding the week's memory verse in your heart and mind. It will require some work, to be sure. But it will be working within the parameters of God's grace, and that will make it engaging and fun.

Before you R.S.V.P., let me give you an overview of what to expect in your six-week excavation. Each day's study includes the following elements:

Focus and Scripture: This opening section is preparation for your heart and mind. I encourage you to take time to worship, pray, and invite the Holy Spirit to make your heart pliable to receive what He has in store for you. He's always eager to help if you ask. That's His role, and it delights Him when you invite Him to open your heart to receive His teaching.

Questions and Prompts: These are scattered throughout the day's content in **purple boldface** type. Some are very basic instructions, such as writing a specific Bible verse. Take time to ponder God's Word as you write and reflect. Others involve deeper research, while still others provide time to pause and praise. Each instruction is designed to help you connect more deeply with the heart of God.

Journal Writing: Though space is provided in this book for responding to questions and prompts, you also may want to express some of your thoughts in a journal where you will have more room to write. If you're not currently keeping a journal, now is a great time to start. I'm certain that if you will be open and listen, God will tell you some pretty awesome things about Himself during the next six weeks, and I encourage you to write these things down in a separate notebook. Journal writing doesn't have to be difficult. Simply share your heart on paper—nothing formal, just heart-talk. My favorite journals are the inexpensive composition books.

"Anonymous" Notes: Scattered throughout the study you'll find notes from some anonymous contemporary women—women much like you and me. These notes are dear to me because they were shared from ordinary women who have deep things on their hearts. I'm so grateful for their offerings and their willingness to share. Their comments and insights will help to reinforce the personal connections and relevance of the anonymous women we are studying.

Today's Touchpoint: This is the daily wrap-up that brings it all together: you, Jesus, and the world. We must allow God's Word to intersect with our daily lives if we want transformation, and this is the purpose of the Touchpoint. You'll notice that some provide activities and others prompt reflection. Either way, I hope you'll hear God's voice speak clearly to you.

Prayer: My friend, I can't tell you the many times I've paused to pray during the writing of this study. I invite you to pray the prayers that close each day's lesson with me in spirit. May your heart be fortified with God's joy with each petition.

As our heavenly Father placed the message of *Anonymous: Discovering the Somebody You Are to God* on my heart, He had you in mind. I'm sure of it! Each of these four nameless women was known and loved by Him, and so are you, my friend. My prayer is that you will explore, grow, and come to enjoy your relationship with God in a richer, deeper way by journeying through this study with me. May you find the joy that comes with knowing *you* are sweetly significant to Jesus.

There you have it—your personal invitation. It's my prayer that you'll accept it, sign the R.S.V.P. on the next page, and become a bona-fide *Anonymous* Bible study girlfriend!

Anonymous Bible Study

R.S.V.P.

_____ accepts with pleasure

(Signature)

_____

(Date)

Week 1
Shades of Anonymous
When You Feel Invisible

Our Story

Whether you turn to the right or to the left, your ears will hear a voice behind you, saying, "This is the way; walk in it."

Isaiah 30:21 NIV

Imagine you are a five-year-old filled with panic at being lost in the crowd. When I was that age, my mother and I were walking on a busy sidewalk in Charlotte, North Carolina, when my hand slipped away from her grasp on me. Immediately sensing the anguish of being un-tethered to security, my eyes focused on the back of a woman twenty feet away. I was sure she was my mom, and I began calling out and running toward her. Halfway there I heard a voice shouting from behind me, saying, "I'm here, Honey. Come back." Hearing my mom's voice quieted my pounding heart and made everything okay. She had never lost sight of me and was calling me back to her side.

My friend, earthly living can leave you feeling lost in the crowd and untethered to security, but there is One calling your name. God loves you and is calling you to walk with Him for the journey that He has planned specifically for you! I'm praying that you will hear Him call!

Our Name: *Known*

This week we begin our study by searching God's heart and exploring our own thoughts about our perception of *anonymous*. What does it look and feel like? How does God long to touch our hearts during those times when we think we are less than we really are? You'll perhaps be reminded of times when you felt nobody knew your name or cared anything about you. You'll also be reminded of others whose stories that have caused them to feel the same. And the good news for all of us is that we are known—and loved—by God!

As we prepare to explore four women from Scripture who had life-changing encounters when they came face to face with Jesus, you'll revisit your own salvation experience or journey of faith. And if you've not yet invited Jesus to be your personal Lord and Savior, you'll have the opportunity to take Him up on His gift of grace during our study time together.

This first week of *Anonymous* is a bit different than the others as it prepares our hearts and minds for digging into the anonymous stories to come. May you find rich blessings ahead!

Memory Verse

[She] who dwells in the secret place of the Most High shall remain stable and *fixed under the shadow of the Almighty.*

Psalm 91:1 Amplified

This is a verse I tucked into my memory files many years ago. I often call it to mind when I need a hefty dose of God's stability to see me through a particular situation. I encourage you to write it on an index card or a note in your phone or tablet so you can keep it near for quick reference. When memorizing Scripture, I *practice* saying it throughout the day. I also call it to mind when I go to bed and when I get up. It's also becoming a sweet experience for me to think over it when I wake up during the night.

When I memorize a new verse or passage, I begin by taking a few words at a time, talking them over with the Lord. For this one, I spent a couple of days considering the phrase, *"[She] who dwells in the secret place of the Most High."* I talked to God about where His secret place is and how I dwell there.

Memorizing Scripture slowly and thoughtfully will help you find personal purpose in its meaning, and that will help you to memorize it!

Day 1: Ever Feel Anonymous?

Focus: God's Deep Love

Scripture:

If I speak in tongues of human beings and of angels but I don't have love, I'm a clanging gong or a clashing cymbal. ²If I have the gift of prophecy and I know all the mysteries and everything else, and if I have such complete faith that I can move mountains but I don't have love, I'm nothing. ³If I give away everything that I have and hand over my own body to feel good about what I've done but I don't have love, I receive no benefit whatsoever.

⁴Love is patient, love is kind, it isn't jealous, it doesn't brag, it isn't arrogant, ⁵it isn't rude, it doesn't seek its own advantage, it isn't irritable, it doesn't keep a record of complaints, ⁶it isn't happy with injustice, but it is happy with the truth. ⁷Love puts up with all things, trusts in all things, hopes for all things, endures all things.

⁸Love never fails. As for prophecies, they will be brought to an end. As for tongues, they will stop. As for knowledge, it will be brought to an end. ⁹We know in part and we prophesy in part; ¹⁰but when the perfect comes, what is partial will be brought to an end. ¹¹When I was a child, I used to speak like a child, reason like a child, think like a child. But now that I have become a man, I've put an end to childish things. ¹²Now we see a reflection in a mirror; then we will see face-to-face. Now I know partially, but then I will know completely in the same way that I have been completely known. ¹³Now faith, hope, and love remain—these three things—and the greatest of these is love.

1 Corinthians 13 CEB

Years ago I was rushing to catch the connecting flight that would take me back to the comforts of my North Carolina home. It had been a sweet event for the ladies who had gathered for the weekend retreat. They had come longing to understand more about what a relationship with Jesus Christ means and how it plays out in daily living. As I left them, I was filled with sweet thoughts of how the Holy Spirit had opened eyes with understanding and filled hearts with hope—*that* plus a bit of anxiety that I might miss my flight. Plane doors were closing as I lighted with a determined bounce outside the pilot's cubby. It didn't even matter where I'd be sitting; I was just grateful that it was on the *inside* of this plane. My relief was soon replaced with an unexpected dousing of melancholy to my spirit.

"We were hoping nobody would sit here." These were the words I heard after I'd joyfully skirted down the aisle and pulled up beside the man and woman on either side of the little perch of a spot that was reserved for me for the flight home. It was a rare moment that left me with absolutely nothing to say. Oh, there were some mental retaliations that sprang to my mind, such as "Thanks for the warm welcome" and "Excuse me, your Highness," and such; but the Holy Spirit simply closed my mouth, and all in all that was a very good thing for that moment. It was good because it got me thinking about how our perception of others can be a negative anchor that plops down and settles within our souls. That was evidenced in my internal reaction to this situation. I had just come away from a fun time with girlfriends where we'd shared the love and hope of Jesus and how His joy is available for every stressful detail of life. For a few sweet days, we had enjoyed navigating the waters of His deep love. And then, with that one comment I seemed to hear, "Drop the anchor; we're going to dock here for a while!"

So, where were we docked? Smack-dab in the middle of hurt feelings and wounded ego, with a little pride swirlin' around—you know, all those feelings that in an instant can take your mind off Jesus and place it on yourself and your own importance. And then, unless you pull up anchor pretty quickly, you'll crouch down deeper in that crud of self-indulgence.

My friend, the purpose of this Bible study is to join you in your travels. Some days we find ourselves in a good place, a place of enjoying God's peace and direction in life. And we want to celebrate together the goodness of God. Other days we find ourselves hunkered down in the crud, and on those days we especially need to approach the welcoming heart of God. He has your spot reserved and longs for you to focus on Him. He wants you to allow His great love for you to override negative circumstances and negative opinions of others. He also wants you to allow Him to pull up any anchor of negativity that has weighed down your soul and clouded your vision of Him. We all have those weights of our past. It's never His plan that you live a life chained to sadness over yesterday. It's also not His plan that you live your today defined by the faulty perceptions of others—especially the perception of being anonymous.

So, let's talk about the concept of feeling anonymous. Here's our working definition for this study:

anonymous – lacking individuality, unique character, or distinction

This first week of our study is designed to get you thinking about the love that God has for you. It's a time of preparing your heart and mind for deep revelation from God. My goal is also to help you begin to identify with these four nameless women straight from the pages of God's Word. Make no mistake about it: although nameless to us, each of these real, anonymous women held a special place in the heart of God. Each of their stories is included in His Word to encourage us and empower us to live life in vibrant relationship with Jesus Christ.

I'm so excited for us to connect during the next weeks. Today's the day to begin preparing your heart to move in holy tandem with these four women who were transformed from being nobodies by earthly circumstantial definition into glorious somebodies in God's marvelous scheme of things.

Let me pray with you:

Dear heavenly Father, thank You that You are the God of the anonymous ones. I know beyond all doubt that You called this study forth in Your holy design for this time and this place. Bless the precious heart of each woman who is reading these words. Give her hope and empower her heart right now to receive the things You have in store for her. I thank You in advance, and I love You. Amen.

Now, to get your mind revolving around the theme of anonymous, respond to the following:
Have you ever felt anonymous (as defined on the previous page)?

Based on what you know about the direction of this study so far, what do you hope to gain from it?

Now, some deeper thoughts . . .
Think of a time when you were hit with a random, sudden distraction that caused you to lose your focus on God's love. It could involve anything. Briefly describe that event.

Is there something or someone from your past that seems to have you anchored to lies about who you are?

Concerning that person or thing, how have you tried to find freedom?

Have you resigned yourself personally and privately to the lie that you can never be completely free from this weight emotionally?

If so, what do you think is the source of this false assumption?

Today's Touchpoint

What would you like to experience in your relationship with your heavenly Father during the upcoming weeks?

Talk to Him about it by writing your thoughts below or in a journal or notebook.

Dear heavenly Father, thank You that Your love is indeed my greatest possession. Keep me determined to reject the lies and remain conscientious about studying and meditating upon Your Word. I know what You say about me is true. Keep me refreshed in that reality. I love You. Amen.

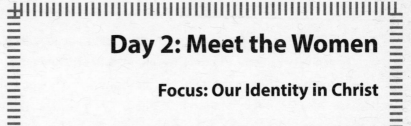

Day 2: Meet the Women

Focus: Our Identity in Christ

Scripture:

Therefore, my brothers and sisters whom I love and miss, who are my joy and crown, stand firm in the Lord.

Loved ones, ²I urge Euodia and I urge Syntyche to come to an agreement in the Lord. ³Yes, and I'm also asking you, loyal friend, to help these women who have struggled together with me in the ministry of the gospel, along with Clement and the rest of my coworkers whose names are in the scroll of life.

⁴Be glad in the Lord always! Again I say, be glad! ⁵Let your gentleness show in your treatment of all people. The Lord is near. ⁶Don't be anxious about anything; rather, bring up all of your requests to God in your prayers and petitions, along with giving thanks. ⁷Then the peace of God that exceeds all understanding will keep your hearts and minds safe in Christ Jesus.

⁸From now on, brothers and sisters, if anything is excellent and if anything is admirable, focus your thoughts on these things: all that is true, all that is holy, all that is just, all that is pure, all that is lovely, and all that is worthy of praise. ⁹Practice these things: whatever you learned, received, heard, or saw in us. The God of peace will be with you.

Philippians 4:1-9 CEB

Over the past several months, I've retreated with four women from the New Testament. Consciously, they've been my companions during the day. And on many nights of light sleep, they've popped on the scene and engaged my mind as I entertained questions about how they felt in their daily lives and what it was like to actually see Jesus in person. It's weirdly true that on many occasions I'd peek at the clock several times during the night, excitedly looking forward to getting up to do more research and record my findings. I've never had a writing experience quite like this one. Somehow our great God just connected our hearts.

If you've experienced this kind of heart-to-heart connection with God's Word, you know firsthand how it transforms your life. If you haven't experienced it but would like to, God will make sure you have it if only you ask Him. God wants the Bible to become alive and engaging to you. It delights Him when you earnestly want to dig deeper and understand His revelations on a personal level. My prayer for you is that the weeks ahead will be a growing-in-knowledge-and-love experience between you and the sovereign God of the universe.

Throughout the study, I'll refer to these anonymous women as our *girlfriends* and *sisters*. That's because this is who they've become to me as I've investigated their lives and talked to our heavenly Father about them. It's the coolest thing how God has lifted them off the pages of Scripture and placed them before me in present-day-neighborhood familiarity. I've considered their plights and how their circumstances could have undone them, but instead, by God's mercy, they came face to face with Jesus.

To help our study along, I've given these women names so that we might identify with them as real people. Each woman's name gives a reference point of *who she was* when she met Jesus. Although their culture, lifestyles, and particular stories may differ from yours, you may realize you share traces of their identities.

Here they are, the women you'll meet through our study. First we'll meet *Judged* in the house of the Pharisee. Then we'll encounter *Hurting* near the shores of the Sea of Galilee. By the well in Samaria we'll be introduced to *Ordinary*. And finally, in Jerusalem's temple courtyard, we'll become acquainted with *Shame*.

We don't know for sure because it's not spelled out in Scripture, but I imagine that *Judged, Hurting, Ordinary,* and *Shame* each faced Jesus with warped identities. In other words, they had become the personification of what they were going through.

Life lends itself to that kind of thinking, you know. If you hurt long enough, you begin to view yourself as a hurting person. If you're never noticed as someone making a contribution or if you're never valued, you begin to perceive yourself as overlooked. Each of these women we'll study had some time to develop scars before she met Jesus. I think that's why I've become so intrigued and connected with them. I've had moments with every one of those scars. Here's the beautiful reality. Having a relationship with Jesus Christ dispels every other identity that holds you hostage. We can, however, cloak ourselves for so long in those false identities that we perceive them to be true.

How about you, my friend? Are there events in your past that have scarred you so deeply that you now mostly identify yourself with that situation? Or maybe something is going on with you today that is distracting you from becoming the real you in Christ. Know this: God does not define you by your current or past struggle. He defines you by who you are in Him. As we go through the weeks ahead, my prayer is that you will let go of any negative situations that you have allowed to define you and that you will come to realize your true identity in Jesus Christ. Let me pray for you right now:

Dear heavenly Father, I lift up to You my sister who is reading these words. You alone know the baggage she carries. I pray that her eyes will be opened to Your healing power and that she will embrace and live fully in her identity that is found in You. Amen.

Circle any words or phrases that might have caused you to take on a negative and false identity:

embarrassing situation	**weight or self-image issue**	**illness**
family trouble	**misbehaving children**	**failure**
judgment of others	**not chosen**	**past sin**

other: _____

With Philippians 4:1-9 as your backdrop, jot some thoughts below or in your journal. Talk to your heavenly Father about how your anxieties sometimes define how you see yourself. Ask Him to show you how to become refreshed in the reality of who you are in Him.

Today's Touchpoint

Are there others you know who could be named *Judged, Hurting, Ordinary,* or *Shame*? Ask the Holy Spirit to bring to mind someone who could use a good dousing of Jesus-love. Then, move forward in obedience to share it!

Afterward, write about your experience in the space below or in a journal or notebook.

Dear Father, I long for Your peace that passes all understanding to take over my heart and mind. I confess, Lord, that many times I've taken on false identities from the world instead of finding my true identity in You. Thank You for speaking to me and reminding me that I'm Yours. I love You. Amen.

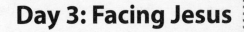

Day 3: Facing Jesus

Focus: Celebrating the Gift of Salvation

Scripture:

God so loved the world that he gave his only Son, so that everyone who believes in him won't perish but will have eternal life.

John 3:16 CEB

Each of the four anonymous women we will study over the next several weeks saw Jesus. I can't tell you how many times during this writing journey I've imagined their individual encounters. The thought of actually looking into the physical face of Jesus, who was fully God and fully man, simply overwhelms me. I invite you right now to begin imagining the beauty of the moment when each of these gals came face to face with the Lord:

Judged faced Approval. *Hurting* faced Healing.
Ordinary faced Remarkable. *Shame* faced Forgiveness.

I imagine the impact of that holy encounter changed their lives forever! I would love to look into the face of the physical Jesus. How about you? Sometimes in my worship moments, I imagine gazing into His eyes and experiencing the penetration of His love as He gazes back into mine. As totally awesome as it would be to see Him in the flesh, Jesus actually said that it is to our benefit that He went away (John 16:7). We are actually living in a more glorious time because He lives on the inside of us!

Oh friend, we must keep our passion fresh! The only way to do this is to return to the basics of God's love. These days I can't meditate enough upon what He did for me on the cross, nor can I over-thank Him for it. One day when I was caught up in talking to Him about how thankful I am, He spoke to my heart. Here's what I heard:

Sometimes you miss the fireworks because you're focused on the sparklers!

Well, my friend, maybe you're like me. Do you sometimes get so caught up in the life around you that you forget Who gave it to you? For the past couple of years, I've made a determined effort to live in thankfulness for what Jesus did for me at Calvary. But even in my determination, I sometimes forget. So, join me as we lift our gaze to the glory of God's fireworks in the gift of our salvation.

God wants you to love Him above anyone or anything else because loving Him puts everything else in perspective. In God you find the hope, peace, and joy that are possible only through a personal relationship with Him. Through His presence in your life you can truly love others, because God is love.

John 3:16 declares, "For God so loved the world that He gave His only begotten Son, that whoever believes in Him should not perish but have everlasting life." John 10:10 records Jesus' statement to us: "I have come that they may have life, and that they may have *it* more abundantly."

A relationship with God begins by admitting you are not perfect but continually fall short of God's standards. Romans 3:23 says that "all have sinned and fall short of the glory of God." The price for our wrongdoings is separation from God. "For the wages of sin is death, but the gift of God *is* eternal life in Christ Jesus our Lord" (Romans 6:23).

God's love comes to you right in the middle of your sin. "But God demonstrates His own love toward us, in that while we were still sinners, Christ died for us" (Romans 5:8). He doesn't ask you to clean up your life first; in fact, you are incapable of doing so. Without His help you simply cannot live by His standards.

Forgiveness begins when you admit your sin to God. When you do, He is faithful to forgive and restore your relationship with Him. "If we confess our sins, He is faithful and just to forgive us *our* sins and to cleanse us from all unrighteousness" (1 John 1:9).

Scripture confirms that this love gift and relationship with God are not just for a special few but for everyone. "For 'whoever calls on the name of the Lord shall be saved'" (Romans 10:13).

Dear sister in Christ, if you have asked for God's gift of salvation, then according to the Scriptures, you have certainly received it. Declare today to be a holy fireworks day of celebration between you and your heavenly Father. Talk to Him about the love gift He has given you. Ask the Holy Spirit to help you not take for granted what cost Jesus His life.

Share some thoughts about what Jesus' sacrifice means to you on a daily basis. Take time to record them below or in a journal.

If you have not yet requested and received God's gift designed purposely and especially for you, you can do so now with the assurance that He is overjoyed to bring you into His family. My dear friend, if you are feeling a nudge of longing, that's His Spirit calling you and inviting you to enjoy His love. The next step is to review the Scriptures listed above and pray the following prayer:

Dear God, I know that I am imperfect and separated from You. Please forgive me of my sin and allow me to be Your child. Thank You for the sacrifice of Your Son, Jesus. I believe He died for my sins, and I want to live my life for You. Amen.

If this is your heartfelt prayer right now, then you can rejoice in your salvation! Remember, you don't have to understand it all; in fact, it's impossible to do so. He only asks that you receive His gift and be faithful to love Him. If you've prayed this prayer to welcome Jesus into your heart for the first time, be sure to share your experience with your group leader, a pastor, or a Christian friend. ***Welcome to God's family, sister!***

I'm so much more thankful for Christ's sacrifice for me than I used to be. It wasn't that I was unappreciative; I just didn't give it much thought. Now I love to think about how and when I invited Him to be my personal Lord and Savior. I often verbally thank Him for what He did on the cross. I also enjoy writing my thankfulness in my journal. Speaking, writing, and singing about Christ's sacrifice keeps it fresh and close to my heart.

Today's Touchpoint

Let's end our study time today with a holy fireworks display! Nothing is more life-changing than our salvation experience. Crossing over from death into life is an event that needs to be celebrated every single day!

Take some time for thought, prayer, and journaling. If you've never written your salvation story, today would be a wonderful time to record it below or in a journal. You also may like to use this time to express your thankfulness in written word to Christ for His sacrifice of love for you. Take care not to rush through this exercise but to truly relish this time of thanking God today.

O, heavenly Father, I want to thank You in a fresh way for giving me life by dying on the cross for me. Forgive me for sometimes acting as though I'm ungrateful. I want to remember Your great sacrifice every day of my life. I love You. Amen.

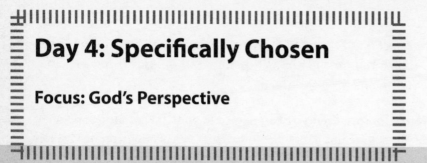

Day 4: Specifically Chosen

Focus: God's Perspective

Scripture:

"You are worthy, our Lord and God,
to receive glory and honor and power,
because you created all things.
It is by your will that they existed and were created."
Revelation 4:11 CEB

The very word *anonymous* implies obscurity and the condition of being unknown. Actually, the four women from Scripture who are the focus of our study were not anonymous at all. God specifically chose them and their stories to be included in His Word.

It may take you by surprise, but God also chose *you* and knew from the beginning that right at this moment you would be reading these words and exploring how your story intersects with His.

You saw me before I was born.
Every day of my life was recorded in your book.
Every moment was laid out
before a single day had passed.
Psalm 139:16 NLT

As you read and reflect on this breathtaking Scripture from the psalmist's pen, I pray that you will catch the gravity of God's heart for you. My friend, you are loved with an incredible love from an extraordinary God! That reality ought to stagger you with wonder and incredulous joy! Look at the riveting words of Jesus to His closest earthly friends shortly before He headed to the cross:

"You did not choose Me, but I chose you and appointed you that you should go
and bear fruit."

John 15:16a

On Day 2 we explored how circumstances often cloud our vision of who we really are in Jesus. Consider this question: *Who did you see in the mirror the last time you looked?*

If you're like many women, you saw the person reflected in your most-recent experience. For instance, if you just yelled at your kids or were short with a coworker, that's the person you saw in the mirror. By the same token, if you recently read a couple of chapters from the Bible and had some wonderful prayer time with the Lord, that person was reflected in your mirror. Our perception of who we are jumps all over the place, doesn't it?

The only way to get an accurate assessment is to look to Jesus, not to ourselves. Unfortunately, many times we follow the world's advice of looking deeply into our souls, trying to discover our identities. My friend, you'll never discover who you are by looking inside yourself but only by looking into the heart of God. I've been in relationship with the Lord for a long time, and I still have to be determined to look to Him and focus on what He thinks instead of looking to myself and others for validation. If we daily remind ourselves it is He who has birthed us, called and chosen us, then we will keep on track. When we forget that, it becomes tempting to bend to the world's opinions and advice.

God does not want any of His children to live an unfulfilled life. He also doesn't want us living lives that do not bear fruit for Him. He has chosen each one of us, you see, not only for salvation but also to play a significant role in His Kingdom's purposes. He has given you a specific personality within a specific set of circumstances. Your circumstances will vary as you progress through life but your calling to be His and to bear fruit for Him will never change.

The four women in Scripture we'll be examining in the upcoming weeks came to Jesus with different backgrounds. *Judged, Hurting, Ordinary,* and *Shame* all brought with them a background that Jesus used to reach others for His glory. When they turned to Him, God used their stories, which included their histories of sin and heartache. Each had an encounter with the Lord that was life changing—not only for themselves, but also for those who would hear their stories.

Listen, my friend: whatever your past, Jesus will use you to shine His glory if you come to Him in repentance. There is never a valid excuse to keep any of us from being effective for Him. The lives of these women from God's Word testify to the fact that He can use smallness, sin, and insignificance of any kind to display His greatness. It is never for us to determine our worth and effectiveness for sharing the love of Jesus. It's only our calling to share it.

Remember, being chosen has everything to do with God; it's not about our worthiness to be called. When the enemy speaks to you of your unworthiness (and he will), the best thing you can do is to agree with him. When I hear his verbal jabs of my unworthiness, here's my response:

> I hear you telling me how unworthy I am, and I totally agree. I was never worthy in the first place to approach God, and I never will be. My access to God and my effectiveness for Him are not based on my worthiness but on what Christ did for me on the cross.

That's why it's vital that we live in awareness of the cross, my friend. Doing so on a daily basis will keep you alert and able to resist the enemy and his schemes.

Now let's look at what it means to be *chosen*. According to the Greek translation of Jesus' words "I chose you" (John 15:16), we are picked out by Him and for Him. For what reason? To bear fruit. Metaphorically speaking this "fruit" is the evidence of His invisible power. The fruit we share is the fruit of the Spirit listed in Galatians 5:22-23 (you will have the opportunity to list the fruit in Today's Touchpoint). The fact that you are called and chosen has nothing to do with your natural abilities. God will use those abilities, to be sure, but the most important aspect is that you were chosen to be in relationship with Him.

It's critical that you not allow any circumstance or person to cause damage to that holy relationship. If that happens, you need to make amends with God as soon as possible by confessing the barrier between you and asking Him to restore your relationship. You see, striving to bear fruit is not what's important. The fruit is the outflow of your love life with Him. The relationship is critical to your walk, your effectiveness, and the daily victories you experience.

It's a common and universal fact that everybody feels anonymous (lacking individuality, unique character, or distinction) at times. These feelings may have to do with how you relate to others or your effectiveness for Jesus. But if you focus on your relationship with Him and His acceptance and love, you will not get caught in the trap of viewing yourself through the lesser lenses of the world around you. And that's some sweet freedom! With you and the Lord sharing a vibrant, close relationship, people and circumstances take on the right perspective—His perspective.

Today's Touchpoint

As we bring today's study to a close, let's consider the characteristics of Christ that are within us.

Turn to Galatians 5:22-23 and list the fruit of the Spirit:

Spend some time reflecting on each of these qualities. Think about how they are evidenced in your personal daily living. The truth is, we cannot produce these characteristics on our own; we can only allow them to radiate from our lives through a deep walk with our Lord.

What is a specific way you feel that God has chosen you to display one or more of His qualities—the fruit of His Spirit?

What are some steps you are willing to take to grow your relationship with Jesus Christ? List them below and describe how you plan to go about making these things reality.

1.

2.

3.

Dear heavenly Father, thank You for my salvation. Because of Your saving grace I can live each day filled with joy and purpose. Put a hunger in my heart, Lord, to live in the fruit of Your Spirit. I want to honor You by allowing others to see You manifested in my life. I love You. Amen.

Day 5: You Are God's Somebody!

Focus: Enjoying Your Place of Honor

Scripture:

To the one who is able to protect you from falling,
and to present you blameless and rejoicing before his glorious presence.

Jude 1:24 CEB

One contemporary anonymous woman shared with me the following painful experience:

I was invited to a special luncheon celebration. Even though I was supposedly an honored guest on that invitation list, I certainly didn't feel like it. After going through the buffet line, I chose my seat at a small table nearby. Every single guest walked right past my table and sat down with others at other tables. I ate my entire meal alone. I felt awkward and very sad that no one wanted to share my company.

~ Anonymous

Does this anonymous note bring to mind a similar personal experience? How did you feel?

How many times have we, as God's children, walked right by someone who needed to feel special? Everybody is Somebody to God. It's my prayer that through our Bible study journey, we will all become much more sensitive to God's longing to reach out in love to those around us.

We don't usually associate any special recognition with the names of John Doe and Jane Doe. In fact, their only notoriety is that they are the *nobodies standing for the somebodies.* These names have been traditionally used as stand-in names until proper identities are discovered. You'll hear them mentioned on the news, read about them in the papers, even find them at dinner parties.

Think of a formal dinner gathering where name cards with the guests' names mark each place of the seating arrangement. "John" and "Jane" reserve the spots for those seats of honor not yet designated.

With the setting of the dinner banquet in mind, I invite you to share the advice Jesus gave before telling the parable of the great feast—my favorite parable of all time. Ever since I ranked it number one on my list of "Jesus stories," it has both humbled and inspired me. Enjoy reading and visualizing the real-life drama that must have unfolded prior to these words of Jesus. Then we'll sift through the verses to find the treasure.

> *When Jesus noticed that all who had come to the dinner were trying to sit in the seats of honor near the head of the table, he gave them this advice: "When you are invited to a wedding feast, don't sit in the seat of honor. What if someone who is more distinguished than you has also been invited? The host will come and say, 'Give this person your seat.' Then you will be embarrassed, and you will have to take whatever seat is left at the foot of the table!*

> *"Instead, take the lowest place at the foot of the table. Then when your host sees you, he will come and say, 'Friend, we have a better place for you!' Then you will be honored in front of all the other guests. For those who exalt themselves will be humbled, and those who humble themselves will be exalted."*

> *Then he turned to his host. "When you put on a luncheon or a banquet," he said, "don't invite your friends, brothers, relatives, and rich neighbors. For they will invite you back, and that will be your only reward. Instead, invite the poor, the crippled, the lame, and the blind. Then at the resurrection of the righteous, God will reward you for inviting those who could not repay you."*

> Luke 14:7-14 NLT

Oh, the skillful communication of Jesus! He had such a way of exposing the arrogance that permeated the religiosity of His day. Ah, but how His words can both sting and comfort our hearts as well. *Sting*, because I, too, have been guilty of overlooking; *comfort*, because I've been the overlooked. Let's take a look at the background of this passage to understand what prompted Jesus' words.

Often after the services on the Sabbath, the Jews would host a meal and invite special guests. As was the case on other occasions, the Pharisees included Jesus on their invitation list that day for the purpose of trapping Him in some way or another. After catching their attention by healing a man with dropsy, Jesus launched into His speech. No doubt He had watched the guests choosing the best seats for themselves, and this provided the perfect backdrop for this divine illustration and the parable that followed (see Luke 14:15-24). Since the Pharisees were familiar with the proverbs of Solomon, He knew they would recall the following passage.

Write Proverbs 25:6-7 below, and then answer the following question.

What does this proverb say to you personally?

Can't you just imagine this scene unfolding? In the distance, the guests were laying claim to the best seats of the house while Jesus had the attention of the few standing before Him. I can picture Jesus' listeners very aware of that blur of selfishness swirling around them as He brought them to sharp focus with His pointed illustration. In His artful style of communicating, Jesus alluded to the Proverbs passage as He painted a word picture of a great supper with guests arriving. When an honorable guest arrived after the choice seats had been taken, the host could not permit the worthy guest to take the lowest place. Because that would be a breach of etiquette, he was left with one choice. He must inform the person occupying the seat of honor, of which he was not entitled, to take the lowest place. He then would invite the distinguished guest to sit in the place of honor, leaving the humiliated guest with a lesson he'd long remember.

The point of the story? Wouldn't it be better to take the lowliest spot in the first place? And then, if your host disagreed with your choice, you'd hear him inviting you to move to a place of higher honor. You'd be respected in the presence of the other guests instead of embarrassed before them. Jesus went on to teach a lesson in humility and love as he addressed the invitation list. He said that by including those on your list who could not typically enjoy such dining pleasure, you'd be sure to receive a future blessing. The idea is to show kindness without expecting your kindness to be returned.

My dear friend, think of it: you never have to be concerned about your place of honor. If you belong to Christ, He has Himself reserved your spot at the most wonderful celebration banquet of all time! If you are in relationship with Him, then you are held in the highest esteem.

In his vision, the apostle John saw and heard angelic choirs singing and praising God because the heavenly wedding celebration was about to take place.

> *Let us be glad and rejoice and give Him glory, for the marriage of the Lamb has come, and His wife has made herself ready. And to her it was granted to be arrayed in fine linen, clean and bright, for the fine linen is the righteous acts of the saints.*
>
> *Then he said to me, "Write: 'Blessed are those who are called to the marriage supper of the Lamb!'"*
>
> Revelation 19:7-9

This *marriage supper* is a glorious celebration of all who are in Christ! Next week we'll be introduced to the first of our four anonymous women. They never would have imagined they'd land on the guest list of such a grand celebration. Never . . . until they met Jesus!

How about *you*, my friend? If you've ever questioned how He feels about you, then it's time for you to celebrate your place of honor in the heart of God!

Today's Touchpoint

As I stated earlier, this is my favorite story from Jesus. There's just something about it that makes me want to say, "Yay, God!" You can always depend on Him to take up for those who feel neglected, dishonored, unimportant, and humiliated. I think we've all felt overlooked in these ways before.

How does the fact that Jesus has a special place of honor reserved just for you bring joy to your heart? Talk with God about it below or in your journal.

In addition to these feelings, what is God revealing to you regarding the attention He would like you to give those around you?

As we look forward to moving deeply into the Scripture passages ahead, join me in praying that God would make our hearts open and sensitive to hearing from Him.

Dear heavenly Father, thank You that all Your children hold a special place in Your heart. Lord, prepare my heart and mind to receive all You want to give me as we work our way through this study. For those areas of my life that need cleansing, I surrender them to You. The hurts that need healing, I offer to You. Help me to be more sensitive to You and to others. I love You. Amen.

Week 1
Video Viewer Guide

• • • • • • • • • • • • • • • • • • • •

You will seek Me and find Me, when you search for Me with all your heart.
Jeremiah 29:13 NKJV

Father, I desire that they also whom You have entrusted to Me **[as Your gift to Me]** *may be with Me where I am.*

John 17:24a Amplified (emphasis added)

Boosts for Your Prayer/Devotion Time

1. Jesus is _____ for you.

2. Have an accountability _____.

3. Scripture _____.

And I will ask the Father, and He will give you another Comforter (Counselor, Helper, Intercessor, Advocate, Strengthener, and Standby), that He may remain with you forever.

John 14:16 Amplified

[She] who _____ in the secret place of the Most High shall remain _____

and _____ under the shadow of the Almighty.

Psalm 91:1 Amplified

_____ _____ with Jesus Christ changes everything.

Week 2
The Woman Who Anointed Jesus
When You Are Judged

Her Story

³⁶Then one of the Pharisees asked Him to eat with him. And He went to the Pharisee's house, and sat down to eat. ³⁷And behold, a woman in the city who was a sinner, when she knew that Jesus sat at the table in the Pharisee's house, brought an alabaster flask of fragrant oil, ³⁸and stood at His feet behind Him weeping; and she began to wash His feet with her tears, and wiped them with the hair of her head; and she kissed His feet and anointed them with the fragrant oil. ³⁹Now when the Pharisee who had invited Him saw this, he spoke to himself, saying, "This Man, if He were a prophet, would know who and what manner of woman this is who is touching Him, for she is a sinner."

⁴⁰And Jesus answered and said to him, "Simon, I have something to say to you."

So he said, "Teacher, say it."

⁴¹"There was a certain creditor who had two debtors. One owed five hundred denarii, and the other fifty. ⁴²And when they had nothing with which to repay, he freely forgave them both. Tell me, therefore, which of them will love him more?"

⁴³Simon answered and said, "I suppose the one whom he forgave more."

And He said to him, "You have rightly judged." ⁴⁴Then He turned to the woman and said to Simon, "Do you see this woman? I entered your house; you gave Me no water for My feet, but she has washed My feet with her tears and wiped them with the hair of her head. ⁴⁵You gave Me no kiss, but this woman has not ceased to kiss my feet *since the time I came in. ⁴⁶You did not anoint My head with oil, but this woman has anointed my feet with fragrant oil. ⁴⁷Therefore I say to you, her sins, which are many, are forgiven, for she loved much. But to whom little is forgiven, the same loves little."*

⁴⁸Then He said to her, "Your sins are forgiven."

⁴⁹And those who sat at the table with Him began to say to themselves, "Who is this who even forgives sins?"

⁵⁰Then He said to the woman, "Your faith has saved you. Go in peace."

Luke 7:36-50

Her Name: *Judged*

Do you see the love story unfolding in this passage? It's deeply emotional and gets right to the very core of the way God loves and forgives. My heart is so moved by the passion of this woman. I picture her with her eyes fixed on Jesus and her heart determined to get to Him. Something had happened to spur her on. Something glorious had given her the guts to burst into the Pharisee's house to carry out her mission of lavishing love upon Jesus. God's love will woo you that way. The accusing stares and judgments whispered about her did not matter at all. All she wanted to do was get to Jesus.

Living in a world tainted with sin and filled with sinners, it's easy to find yourself trapped inside walls of judgment. And if you're not mindful, you can get caught up in helping to erect those walls around others. I'm excited about our week ahead. We'll talk about deep love and explore grace and forgiveness. With God's holy magnifier, we'll look deeply into His Word to understand how His love can override the careless talk of others. Whether a victim of judgment or an occasional whisperer, Jesus has a pertinent word for all of us straight from His spot at the Pharisee's table.

Memory Verse

A broken spirit is my sacrifice, God.
You won't despise a heart, God, that is broken and crushed.

Psalm 51:17 CEB

Tuck this verse inside your heart and mind this week as a reminder of your sweet offering to your Lord. May its truth fill you with fresh adoration for the One who finds you irresistible, and His is the opinion that counts!

Day 1: The Great Love of God

Focus: Believing God Loves You

Scripture:

[36]*Then one of the Pharisees asked Him to eat with him. And He went to the Pharisee's house, and sat down to eat.* [37]*And behold, a woman in the city who was a sinner, when she knew that Jesus sat at the table in the Pharisee's house, brought an alabaster flask of fragrant oil,* [38]*and stood at His feet behind Him weeping; and she began to wash His feet with her tears, and wiped them with the hair of her head; and she kissed His feet and anointed them with the fragrant oil.*

Luke 7:36-38

I'm a daddy's girl; always have been, always will be. I wrote this dedication to him in one of my books:

> My dad taught me how to enjoy life at an early age. He always had time to play one more game and tell one more story. I treasure the memories of playing Blind Man's Bluff and I Spy . . . night after night after night. Thank you, Daddy, for teaching me the critical life skills of laughter and celebration. You gave me all I needed when I was a child to enjoy life as an adult![1]

I don't normally share about our father-daughter relationship with the women at events where I speak. It hurts me to realize that for many—perhaps you—the word *dad* or *daddy* conjures up feelings of pain, abuse, or disapproval. I would never wish to lead you down that path to unpleasant memories.

However, I was recently reminded of something. God allows in each of our lives earthly experiences to teach us spiritual truths. For me one of these experiences has been the blessing of a dad who loved me, enjoyed being with me, and approved of me. No matter what others thought, he thought I was the best! Throughout my life at home, through my college years, and through my "getting married and raising kids" years, he always wanted to know how I was feeling, what I was involved in, and what was next. During the years of my ministry, he kept my traveling schedule in his Bible so he could pray over the events and "keep watch" over his little girl.

Of all the treasured memories I have of him, the one that just melts my heart is the recollection of him waiting for me to come and visit during the last days we shared together on earth. Approaching his assisted living center, I'd see him there perched in his wheelchair, holding his arms out for a big hug. With a big smile on his face, he was always welcoming, always loving, always wanting to spend time with me.

Every girl needs a daddy like that.

My friend, maybe you're one of the few who share my blessing of this kind of father-daughter relationship. But if this scenario seems totally foreign to you, I have some great news.

You have exactly that kind of Father. He is your Father God, and He's right here welcoming you, loving you, and wanting to spend time with you. Every dream you've ever had of a strong and encouraging dad who loves you unconditionally is within your reach. God adores you. The freeing part is that His love is not based on your success or accomplishments—or even on your worthiness to be loved. Not at all. It's all about Him, you see. He loves you because He created you. *You*, my friend, are the product of His mind, His heart, and His awesome love. Talk about some good news! And it's good news for each one of us, regardless of the kind of father-daughter relationship we've experienced on earth.

As surely as I write this, I know there are some reading these words who *still* feel you are somehow excluded from this kind of perfect love. "Not me," you say. "It's too good to be true." Oh how right you are. It is too good to be true, and that's what makes it all the more wonderfully exciting!

Check the statements below that have described your thoughts about God's love for you. *I feel more loved by God when:*

__ **I feel good about myself.**
__ **I go to church and read my Bible.**
__ **I spend time praying for others.**
__ **I do good things for other people.**
__ **I have my quiet time with Him.**

Can you think of others?

As we dive into today's Scripture, you'll find a perfect example of one who had *no earnings* to bring to Jesus. No, her favor with Him was birthed in passionate, bold love. As we move through the passage this week, you'll see this is the love God longs for from you.

My friend, if you are feeling judged, as this woman certainly was, my prayer is that you will find encouragement and refreshment in the Word of God. I pray her example will spur you on to love

Him all the more. His great mercy trumps every judgmental thought from those around you. I pray your focus will turn from what others think to what He thinks. His opinion is the important one.

Okay, here we go—stepping inside the house of the Pharisee.

> *Then one of the Pharisees asked Him to eat with him. And He went to the Pharisee's house, and sat down to eat.*
>
> Luke 7:36

The home of the Pharisee was a great place for this showdown between love and grace. In this setting, you'll see compassion rather than rules, mercy instead of legalities, and uncompromising love instead of hard-core law. Luke doesn't tell us why Simon invited Jesus over, only that He did. Perhaps Simon was gathering information, wanting to learn more about Jesus and His ways.

Turn to John 3 and name the Pharisee who *did* have a genuine desire to learn more about Jesus.

Unlike Nicodemus, Simon could have been orchestrating an opportunity to accuse Jesus, as the Pharisees did in Luke 6:7. Or perhaps Simon didn't feel strongly either way and was simply curious about the One who was stirring up controversy with His radical love. Whatever the case, I bet he wasn't at all prepared for what was about to go down.

Lo and behold, here she came—the woman in the city who was known as a sinner. The Greek word for *sinner* in this context is *hamartōlos*, a word that means "devoted to sin."[2] This description would have been used by the Pharisees and others to describe women of ill repute. Judged and shunned, she was given dirty looks by perhaps all who passed her on the street. Most likely she was cited as an example of the wrong way to live life. It's likely that no one saw any good in her at all—no one except Jesus.

Take a few moments right now to consider someone who is not highly thought of by most people you know. Does realizing that Jesus has a tender heart of compassion toward this person change your view? Explain.

As she approached Him, Jesus welcomed her. Thank goodness He enjoys keeping company with sinners! He understood the curious attraction she had for Him. Undoubtedly she had heard the good news that if she came to Him in repentance, He would not turn her away. And He didn't.

The longer she was in His presence, the deeper was her expression of love. She lingered before Him, adoring Him by washing His feet with her tears and drying them with her hair. He allowed her to do what she'd come to do: worship Him. And so she did—wholeheartedly and unashamedly. Judged by others but loved by Jesus.

What does Romans 5:8 say about God's love for sinners?

But God shows his love for us, because while we were still sinners Christ died for us. (Romans 5:8 CEB)

Perhaps she'd been out on the streets and within earshot when Jesus had stopped and talked to the crowd about love. Maybe she had talked with Him personally about being forgiven and turning from a lifestyle of sin. Whatever had prompted this bold act of love was huge. Without invitation from Simon, she made her way to Jesus with the gifts of her oil, her tears, and her love.

Biblical commentators state that this alabaster flask of oil was probably costly for her. The container and the perfume were quite exquisite and expensive.

Why do you think she brought this quality of a gift to Jesus?

It must have taken a lot of tears to wash His feet and then dry them with her hair. Evidently her tears flowed profusely.

Can you identify with this kind of weeping before the Lord? If so, explain.

This kind of love was on a whole new plane than the sordid kind she'd found with the men who had fueled her profession. In Jesus, she experienced authentic love, and she knew it!

My heart has been so moved by the passion of this woman. As I've pored over this passage, tears have filled my eyes time and again. She had been released from bondage; so have I. She was so freed by the forgiveness of her sin that her body and soul moved in praise and worship to the One Who had set her free. Everything in me wants to love Jesus like that.

I believe every detail of this encounter between this nameless woman and Jesus is significant. For one, the fact that she was nameless is very gracious, don't you think? Her name does not go down in history associated with her sin. We remember how she loved instead of who she was. There are differing opinions among Bible scholars about her identity, but the truth is that we do not know for certain who this woman was.

What are your thoughts about her remaining anonymous to us?

Another detail that impresses me is that she was the one to wash the feet of Jesus. In the Jewish culture, it was customary hospitality for the host to greet the guest with a welcoming kiss and then wash his feet. In the Pharisee's house, the foot washing was most likely done by the servant. The fact that these common courtesies were left undone leaves us to believe that Simon was not treating Jesus as an honored guest.

Read the account of Jesus washing His disciples feet in John 13:1-17. What was He teaching them through His example?

Picture Jesus propped up on one elbow as He reclined at the table. The woman approached Him from behind. Evidently she had arrived for the purpose of honoring Him by anointing His feet with oil. Now, pause for a moment and see her stopped there behind Him. Because I have the heart of a woman who loves Jesus, I can imagine what happened next. It seems that something triggered her crying, for she "stood at His feet behind *Him* weeping; and she began to wash His feet with her tears, and wiped *them* with the hair of her head; and she kissed His feet and anointed *them* with the fragrant oil" (Luke 7:38).

Perhaps the weight of her past and the forgiveness Jesus offered prompted her weeping. But I also can imagine that her tears might have been motivated in part by the shocked surprise of her precious Lord's feet not being washed, causing tears of sad longing to fill her heart and splash onto His dirty feet. Whatever the reason for her passionate display, she had no water or towel, only teardrops and hair to complete her mission. How moved Jesus must have been by the depth of her love!

Today's Touchpoint

There's nothing that restores my balance and calms my nerves like worshiping Jesus. It's so easy to get caught up in a swirl of nonproductive thinking and behaving. For me, the best way of coming against these earthly attacks is to get alone with Jesus. Visualizing our new biblical girl-friend encountering the Lord has been sweet and worshipful for me. What a joy it has been to discover how she loved Jesus so deeply. Sometime today, I'd like for you to imagine this scene with you being the sinner approaching Jesus with a heart full of love. This may be a new kind of worship experience for you, but give it a try.

Later, share some thoughts in writing below or in your journal.

Dear heavenly Father, thank You so much for including this anonymous woman's story in Your Book. Help me to love You like she loved You. May I be so moved by what You've done for me that my heart overflows with love for all to see. I love You. Amen.

Day 2: How Jesus Views Judgment

Focus: Holding Lightly the Opinions of Others

Scripture:

39Now when the Pharisee who had invited Him saw this, he spoke to himself, saying, "This Man, if He were a prophet, would know who and what manner of woman this is who is touching Him, for she is a sinner."

40And Jesus answered and said to him, "Simon, I have something to say to you."

So he said, "Teacher, say it."

41"There was a certain creditor who had two debtors. One owed five hundred denarii, and the other fifty. 42And when they had nothing with which to repay, he freely forgave them both. Tell Me, therefore, which of them will love him more?"

43Simon answered and said, "I suppose the one whom he forgave more."

And He said to him, "You have rightly judged."

Luke 7:39-43

I'm a crier. My tears are usually precipitated by events that either signify loss, such as when pets die, or extreme joy, such as the births of our grandbabies. Sometimes my tears gush forth from a mixture of both, such as when our sons got married and left home. The deep loss I felt was accompanied by a refreshing joy that there would now be girls in our family. Tears of sadness joined forces with the tears of happiness in such a way I didn't even know *why* I was crying.

And then there are those times when there seems to be no reasonable trigger at all for my sudden tear-burst. Whether it's due to the accumulation of daily stress or to a mind that can't possibly garner one more piece of useful information to be stored, having a good cry just ends up being a very cleansing thing to do! However, for those times my tears are a byproduct of some heartbreak, a particular event from my early teen years usually comes to mind. It was one of those "worst days of my life," which teenage girls are prone to have. I was crouched beside my bed caught up in the throes of depression over the latest junior high drama when my brother heard my sobbing and came to my bedroom. He knocked lightly on the door as he peeked in. "Do you know that God is crying right now because you're hurting so much?" he said. That word of comfort did a lot to relieve my distress of the moment. But much greater than that relief was the truth that put down roots in my heart that day: *My tears matter to God!*

I can remember being very concerned with the judgment of others during my teen years. Having also been a teacher of middle school girls, I can verify the fact that being concerned about what others think of you at that age ranks right up there with who you're going to marry one day! In fact, concern about the opinions of others is something we often carry with us into adulthood.

Grab your dictionary (or search the web) and write one of the definitions given for the word *judgment*:

I have a confession to make. It still matters way too much what others think of me. There are particular areas of my life where my focus still gravitates more toward *what people think* instead of *what God thinks*. How about you?

Circle areas below where you experience this struggle:

behavior of children   social status   education

where I live   intellect   popularity

accomplishments   talents   usefulness in church

past sins   home furnishings   house cleaning

other: _____

Consider this definition of judgment: "the forming of an opinion, estimate, notion, or conclusion, as from circumstances presented to the mind."[3]

Looking at Luke 7:39, write in your own words the Pharisee's assessment of the woman who had entered his house.

Was he ever full of judgment! He was not only offended at what this sinner-woman was doing; he most likely was irritated that it was happening in *his* house. According to Scripture, do you think he still wondered if Jesus could be a prophet? If the setting, his home, had been one of congeniality, it was quickly shifting gears with this new development.

I love sinking into Scripture, and I really get pumped when I get to that strategic moment when Jesus prepares to pounce. This is one of those grand occasions when He uses questioning skills, story illustration, and critical thinking to get His truth across. Wow, what a teacher!

Take note of this interesting tidbit in verse 39. Did Simon audibly pose a question to Jesus?

_____ yes   _____ no

What do you conclude by reading verse 40?

Yep, by now Simon's wheels were turning, and he was becoming really curious about this man, this situation, and what Jesus had to say. As always Jesus spoke with finesse. This time, it was in the parable of two debtors.

Reread Jesus' story in Luke 7:41-43 and then answer the following questions:

Who do you think the lender in the story represents?

Who do you think the debtor who owed a large amount represents?

Who do you think the debtor who owed a small amount represents?

What was the question Jesus asked?

What was the answer Simon gave?

Analyzing the phrase *I suppose* in the Greek, I find the English translation of this sentence might read, "I take it that the one whom he forgave loved more." It suggests that Simon answered rather indifferently, showing that he thought the question was a rather trivial one. But it was not. Jesus never wastes words or circumstances.

Tomorrow we'll explore the message behind this parable, for there's a great teaching ahead. For now, simply notice that Jesus rushed in to affirm Simon's assessment of the storyline. He said, "You have rightly judged" (Luke 7:43b). Simon didn't know it, but with his own words he had just pronounced judgment upon himself.

My sister, all of us struggle from time to time with how others perceive us. It's natural that we do. It's also true that we don't want to toss the opinions of others out the window. It matters much that we behave like Christ. Paul instructs us in Ephesians 5:1 to be imitators of God.

With the Holy Spirit's guidance, we have the responsibility to guide and influence each other in God's ways. So, I'm not talking about the opinions of others in those situations. I'm speaking of the insecurities brought on by feelings of judgment and negative evaluations by others. God does not want us to become overly concerned with impressing others. He also does not want us to allow the judgments of others, whether accurate or not, to consume us.

God has given us strong words about judgment. Using a print or online Bible concordance, find verses related to judging others (look up the words *judge* and *judged*). Write two verses that stand out to you.

There are so many situations where we might face judgment from others. For instance, we are now living in the grand age of social media. This term refers to the various interactions among people in the virtual realm.

How do you think the verses above about judging others apply within the social media realm? Can you give an example?

This entire topic of *feeling judged* and *judging others* can be quite convicting, right? As I've researched and talked with the heavenly Father about this, I have been nudged by His Spirit more than once about my attitudes. He has shown me areas where I've been preoccupied with the thoughts of others. He also has brought to light those times when I've been the guilty one, passing judgment when I had no business doing so. I'll have to say, although painful at times, I'm very thankful for His Word that purifies me and helps me to become more like Him.

Today's Touchpoint

Review the definition of judgment given earlier: *the forming of an opinion, estimate, notion, or conclusion, as from circumstances presented to the mind.*

It's important to remember that those who judge us are doing so with their own conclusion from facts that have been deposited in their minds. Now, their assessment may be accurate. For example, Simon the Pharisee's evaluation of the sinful woman's character was right on. Did Jesus applaud him for judging her correctly? Of course not. Just because someone has the details of a situation down pat does not give that person permission to pass judgment.

Place yourself in the sandals of *Judged*, our girlfriend from Scripture. To me, it's quite obvious that her tears of love were mingled with tears of regret and shame. The heart of Jesus Christ graciously received every penitent sob she released. Her tears were not wasted or of no value; they were dear to Him. They represented intense sorrow and repentance.

Her heart's message could have been the same as the psalmist's: "You have seen how many places I have gone. Put my tears in Your bottle" (Psalm 56:8 NLV).

I'm so thankful that every tear I've ever cried matters to God, aren't you?

If you are living with judgment from others concerning a sin in your life, pause right now and give it to your heavenly Father for safe keeping. If you have yet to confess this sin, you may do so right now.

Read 1 John 1:9 and then write it on an index card or a note in your phone or tablet to carry with you. On the back of the card or at the bottom of the note in your phone or tablet, reword this verse into the following prayer:

Dear Father, I'm confessing my sin of _____ to You right now. Thank You for Your faithfulness in being the Fair Judge. Thank You for forgiving me and cleansing me from unrighteousness. Amen.

On a second card or note, write the verse Micah 7:19. On the reverse side of the card or at the bottom of the note, reword this verse to voice your own prayer of thanksgiving to Jesus.

What about those times when you are judged because of faulty information, gossip, and lies? Don't you dare allow a foothold of bitterness in your heart toward those people who judge and accuse you. Here are two strategies that will honor God and bring relief to you:

1. Rejoice in who you are in Christ.
2. Leave your accusers with Jesus.

Make no mistake: He will deal with them in His time and in His way.

Dear heavenly Father, thank You for such practical advice from Your Word. I'm learning so much about how You want me to live victoriously. Keep me mindful of applying Your truth found in Scripture to my daily circumstances. I long to be more caught up in You and less concerned about the judgments of others. Show me how to do this. Thank You for keeping track of my tears, and thank You for loving me. Give me energy and holy insight to love You more. Amen.

Day 3: Jesus Our Defender

Focus: Changed by Love

Scripture:

[44]Then He turned to the woman and said to Simon, "Do you see this woman? I entered your house; you gave Me no water for My feet, but she has washed My feet with her tears and wiped them with the hair of her head. [45]You gave Me no kiss, but this woman has not ceased to kiss My feet since the time I came in. [46]You did not anoint My head with oil, but this woman has anointed My feet with fragrant oil."

Luke 7:44-46

Yesterday we took a look at the first part of the dialogue between Jesus and the Pharisee. Things were going pretty smoothly for ol' Simon, but Jesus was about to turn the tables on this conversation.

Reread verses 41-43 of Luke 7 (see page 39). What was the question Jesus asked Simon when He finished telling the story about the two debtors?

Way too easy a question with an obvious answer. Upon instructing him to look at the woman, Jesus moved in for the kill. Here's my paraphrase:

> *Simon, just look at this woman! Although you invited me to your house today, you didn't welcome me with a basin of water and towel to wash my feet. She has washed them with her outpouring of tears and dried them with the hair on her head. You didn't offer a kiss of hospitality, but she hasn't stopped kissing my feet since I came in. And you did not show respect by anointing my head with oil as you do for many other guests, but she has lavished her fragrant oil all over my feet.*

What a contrast between the well-to-do righteous man and the lowly sinner. With verbal gusto Jesus spoke to Simon but also exposed to those gathered the shabby treatment He'd received from His host. He had not been met with any of the customary protocol for honored guests. At best, His reception had been inhospitable.

Although Jesus spoke strongly, I don't believe He spoke harshly, do you? His grace is too inclusive for that. We don't know Simon's true motives for inviting Jesus over, but Jesus knew exactly what was in his heart. Whatever the Pharisee's objective, Jesus took the opportunity to teach deep spiritual truth. His words were for Simon, as well as for the other guests who were invited that day.

Search the Gospels. Can you name others who were seeking Jesus? (Matthew 2, Luke 19, John 3 will get you started.) Write a few names or identifiers below.

Jesus invited such encounters! Knowing the motive of each seeker's heart, He longed to reveal His nature and love.

According to his heart's response, Simon seemed embarrassed by the woman of ill repute and her actions in his home. He simply did not comprehend her apparent joy over her regeneration. It did not occur to him that she had experienced forgiveness and was overwhelmed with love. Remember his thoughts: *If Jesus knew what kind of woman this was he would not allow her to touch Him.*

I imagine his enlightenment came slowly as Jesus made His way through the telling of His story. I believe Simon gradually understood the point Jesus was making with the moneylender and debtors. I think he caught the inference in the story to himself and to the woman.

State in your own words the truth hidden in the parable of the two debtors:

We don't know for certain the answer to the next question, because the Scriptures don't follow up with Simon's response to Jesus. So, at this point, let's enjoy a bit of *biblical conjecture*. It's okay to do that, you know. In fact, I find it quite spiritually exhilarating. We'll explore this concept more in depth a little later in the study, but for now simply share your thoughts on the following:

Do you think Simon became a follower of Jesus? Explain your answer.

To sum up the facts as we know them:

- The host had given Jesus no water; the woman poured water from her eyes, flowing from her heart.
- The host had not greeted Jesus with a kiss on the cheek; the woman humbly kissed His feet.
- The host had not anointed Jesus with oil; the woman poured precious perfume on His feet.

Isn't it interesting to think of how Simon saw himself as a righteous and God-fearing man who had it all together, religiously speaking? Truth is, he was a sinner needing God's grace. It's evident he saw this woman as a much bigger sinner than himself. The situation holds a bit of irony in that the woman, who was a notorious sinner, was actually in a better position spiritually speaking than Simon. She knew she needed forgiveness, and she received it. As for Simon, his self-righteousness blinded him. We can only hope that later on he came to the same realization that she did.

Skim again Luke 7:36-50. Do you see any words spoken by the woman?

_____ Yes   _____ No

Sometimes the best words are those spoken within the heart. Her actions certainly conveyed her thoughts—perhaps better than any words could have.

> *Don't be quick with your mouth or say anything hastily before God, because God is in heaven, but you are on earth. Therefore, let your words be few.*
> Ecclesiastes 5:2 CEB

Perhaps the reason she did not speak was because there seemed to be no verbiage to convey her gratitude. Bursting into tears was the action that conveyed her joy of forgiveness.

Can you recall an experience of being so overwhelmed that there were no words adequate to express your thoughts? If so, describe it below:

Using a print or online concordance, look up the words *silent* and *silence*. Choose one of the Scripture references and describe a personal situation that applies to that particular verse.

There's another detail of this account that fascinates me, and it's one I've thought about quite often. Jesus was not only her Savior; He was her Defender. This woman had been forgiven her sins, and she wanted to thank Him. Because of the grace she'd received, she wanted to bring a gift to Jesus. She didn't ask permission; she would have been denied. She didn't seek approval of others, only Him. She loved deeply because she had been loved deeply. With humility and gratitude, she made her way to her Lord. And Jesus was all about defending her—publicly and straight to her heart.

Another love story with striking similarities comes to mind; I guess we women know how to love, right? This is a passage with another nameless woman. Although Bible students disagree on her identity, what is not in question is her extravagant love for Jesus.

Read Matthew 26:6-13. Then answer the following questions.

What was her gift to Jesus?

What comment did Jesus' disciples make?

Summarize Jesus' comments to them in your own words.

In Matthew 26:10 Jesus says, "Why are you bothering this woman?" (NIV). I love this line! It has become one of my all-time favorite Jesus statements. You may enjoy taking a few moments to search this verse out in other translations. Whichever ones you read, the truth shouts valiantly: *When we move in love and obedience to our Lord, He rushes to defend us against our accusers.* These accusers come in a variety of ways. They may be:

- Relational—People not understanding the things you do because of your love for Jesus.
- Situational—Being in a job or circumstance that comes against His peace and security.
- Mental—Negative self-talk that undermines your confidence.
- Evil (the accuser)—Doubts, fears, worries, guilt, and the like.

Briefly describe an experience you've had with one of these accuser scenarios.

Now, hear Jesus' whisper over your accuser: *Why are you bothering this woman?* How does this make you feel?

My friend, I cannot put into words the impact His *whisper of defense* has had on my spiritual stamina. I've trained myself to seek out His voice over the din of the accusing one. Grabbing hold of this practice, sister, will keep you walking in victory!

> So, what do you think? With God on our side like this, how can we lose? If God didn't hesitate to put everything on the line for us, embracing our condition and exposing himself to the worst by sending his own Son, is there anything else he wouldn't gladly and freely do for us?
>
> Romans 8:31 *The Message*

Today's Touchpoint

What a beautiful week we've had exploring extravagant love for our Lord. I want to remind and encourage you that *growing in love with Christ* is a process. It's gradual and takes time. Look at the following anonymous note.

I don't feel like I love Jesus as much as I should. Some Christians around me seem to have so much passion and excitement about their love for Him. I just don't feel that way. Is something wrong with me?

~ Anonymous

If you've ever had similar feelings, or if you feel this way now, take heart. Don't let that accuser throw you down. If your desire is to grow more deeply in love with Jesus, you can do so by reaching out to Him in faith. There have been many times in my life when I've lifted my heart and hands upward, saying, "Lord, I don't know how to love You with my whole heart, soul, mind, and strength, but I sure want to. Will You teach me?" Each time I've genuinely prayed that prayer of longing, I've sensed an overwhelming joy that seems to spill right out of God's own heart into mine. He's pleased to give us our heart's desire when that desire is all about loving Him. And the beauty of it all is that each step along the way brings joy to Him and fulfillment to you.

As we come to the end of today's lesson, my prayer is that you are longing to love Jesus more. If so, begin today to make the following commitments:

- Schedule a daily time for worshiping Him. For my personal worship time, I enjoy singing, sometimes with music and sometimes without. I also enjoy dancing in praise to Him.
- Set aside a daily time to get to know Him through Scripture study.
- Simply enjoy being quiet in His presence, and do it many times during the day.

My friend, these are suggestions; these things work for me. God created you with a special brand of unique longing for Him. He will show you how to deepen your intimacy if you ask Him. It blows me away to remember the place of the ultimate essence of extravagant love: the cross of Christ. That love He manifested was absurd, nonsensical, and reckless. There was simply no reason other than *love* that motivated the Son of God to willingly give up His earthly life so that we might enjoy a love relationship with Him forever. May our world be so rocked by this gift that everything in us rushes to love Him back!

Lord Jesus, I do love You, but I want to love You more. Please light a fire in my heart to love You with my entire body, soul, mind, and strength. Lord, I pray that You'll draw me into Your Word so that I can more fully understand Your extravagant love for me, which You displayed on the cross. Help me to hear Your love words whispered into my heart, instead of the words of my accusers. Thank You for instructing me today through Your Spirit. With gratitude and a humble heart, I give You my love. Amen.

Day 4: The Law of Love

Focus: Being Freed from Seeking Approval

Scripture:

47"Therefore I say to you, her sins, which are many, are forgiven, for she loved much. But to whom little is forgiven, the same loves little."

48Then He said to her, "Your sins are forgiven."

Luke 7:47-48

Jesus saw this woman as a *forgiven* sinner. Speaking to Simon, Jesus did not name her sins or make light of them; He merely stated that there were many of them and they were forgiven. Her sins were not forgiven because she loved much; that would have come by her forgiveness. Rather, she loved much because her sins had already been forgiven. This was evidenced in her outpouring of love to Jesus. As we saw in Day 2, within this account lies the illustration of how two debts were canceled without any work on the debtors' part (vv. 41-43). Perhaps there were other words between Jesus and Simon, but what we know from the sharing of the parable is that Jesus was inviting Simon to acknowledge and confess his sins so that he also could experience much joy through the cleansing of God's grace and forgiveness.

Later in the study we'll discuss in greater depth how the Pharisees were caught up in rules and regulations. They seemed to live in such fear of offending God that everything they did revolved around making sure they didn't. Their lists of things to do and things not to do were devised in order to win and keep the approval of God. It's not uncommon for modern day Christians to tiptoe down that same path from time to time. So, let's examine more closely the idea of winning God's approval as it relates to our salvation and our love relationship with Him.

1. Earning God's approval in order to receive salvation

Take a look at these verses and answer the following questions.

For by grace you have been saved through faith, and that not of yourselves; it is the gift of God.

Ephesians 2:8

For God so loved the world that He gave His only begotten Son, that whoever believes in Him should not perish but have everlasting life.

John 3:16

Who gives the gift of salvation?

What is our part in it?

Sometimes, my friend, we just need to be reminded of the basic and glorious truth of salvation by faith alone! Is there any other area of life in which you do *not* have to work at earning some kind of approval? In almost every part of life, we're evaluated in some way. It may be by performance, intelligence, creativity, personality, appearance, or some other measure. We're so conditioned to the idea of earning approval that it's difficult to grasp that God does not evaluate us by our efforts.

For we are God's handiwork, created in Christ Jesus to do good works, which God prepared in advance for us to do.

Ephesians 2:10 NIV

Whose handiwork are we?

Where is this handiwork created?

Why did God create us?

Who has authored these good works for us to do?

Salvation is God's gift to us and for us, so that we might live in deep intimacy with Him and "explode" His glory throughout the world. Our extravagant love becomes the consequence or result of our salvation; it is not the cause of it.

2. Earning God's approval in order to retain salvation

I cannot think of any more miserable existence for a child of God than doubting God's salvation. In fact, this is one of my spiritual hot spots. It just grieves me deeply when *those who have received salvation from God by faith* wrestle with worries about losing that same salvation. For the child of God, thoughts of losing your salvation are a tool of the enemy to keep you distracted and nonproductive for Jesus.

Have you or anyone you've known ever struggled with worries about losing your salvation? Describe the feelings that accompanied this struggle.

Since this is not uncommon in the Christian community, let's stake our claim on the authority of God's Word. If you love and follow Jesus Christ as your Lord and Savior, you and your salvation are 100 percent safe and secure in Him!

Go back to John 3:16 and read it slowly, meditating upon each word.

Truth: *You are blood related.*

The moment you believed in Jesus and accepted Him as your Savior, you became God's child and He became your heavenly Father. This was made possible through the shed blood of Jesus on the cross. You were brought into the Kingdom by faith in the blood of Christ shed on the cross for you, and His blood guarantees that relationship. What's true in the physical world with blood relatives is true in the spiritual world, but in a deeper and greater way. My brother and I are biologically related, having the same parents. I do not stop being his sister if I stop talking to him for a while or if I do things that displease him. The same is true with God's family. If you are in it, you cannot drop out by something you might do or not do. Just as you become a part of God's family by faith, so you remain in God's family by faith. God's grace is the guarantee—not your actions.

Truth: *Jesus has you covered.*

Those who follow Jesus cannot be snatched out of His saving hand. To suggest so casts doubt on the safe grasp of our Savior. Look at what He said.

> *My sheep hear My voice, I know them, and they follow Me. I give them eternal life, and they will never perish—ever! No one will snatch them out of My hand."*
>
> John 10:27-28 HCSB

Truth: *Jesus' sacrifice has already covered every sin, and it is by faith in this sacrifice that we receive God's gift of salvation.*

In the Book of Hebrews we read that "[Christ] entered the most holy place once for all, not by the blood of goats and calves, but by His own blood, having obtained eternal redemption" (9:12 HCSB). Christ died once for every sin. And because we are saved by grace through faith in this ultimate and final sacrifice, salvation is a gift that we receive—not earn (again, see Ephesians 2:8).

My friend, if you have invited Jesus Christ to be your Lord and Savior and have received the gift of salvation, it is a matter of faith and trust that you never again doubt your salvation. Doubting your salvation is essentially dismissing Christ's death and resurrection. It's like saying, "Lord, I know You said that You died once for me and that with Your sacrifice I have been saved from sin, but..."

You see, anytime you step away from the truth of Christ's gift of salvation, you are adding *your works* to God's grace. You're accepting His grace but adding a bit of you to the mix. On this the Scriptures are clear: Faith in God's gift of grace is sufficient—not only for receiving salvation but also for keeping it!

3. Earning God's approval in your daily walk

In the Old Testament, before Christ came, the law required God's people to atone or make payment for their own sins. Thank goodness we live on this side of the cross! Under the law, God related to humanity through commandments and regulations. Under grace, God relates to us through faith in the shed blood of Jesus Christ.

Oh, there is such sweetness in the Lord's words to our dear sister who lovingly showered Him with her devotion. He could have voiced many things to her, such as specifying her sins or reiterating the fact that she had many of them. He could have given her specific instructions about her actions from there on out. But Jesus merely said to *Judged*, "Your sins are forgiven." There was no list of do's and don'ts for her to follow in order to earn His love and approval.

Being transparent and honest, I join the ranks of many who have grappled with earning God's approval. I've often described myself as being a new covenant gal living in an old covenant prison. I'm not talking about salvation issues but about feeling loved and approved of by God. Can you relate?

Place a check beside the things you've done in an attempt to earn God's approval.

_ attended church services   _ given money for a church project

_ made meals for a family in need   _ joined Bible study groups

_ helped with a missions project   _ read your Bible

_ written a note of encouragement

_ visited a shut-in

Can you add others?

Now, stay with me here. You could do all of the above out of love for God, having nothing to do with trying to gain His favor. It's all about the motive of your heart. The longer I walk with Christ, the more I'm prompted to reach out in love to others in His name. It's rare that I find myself explicitly doing things to win His approval. In fact, I can safely say that winning God's approval seldom enters my thinking these days. That's not to my credit, but to His. The longer and closer we walk with Him, the more He redirects our focus to His way of thinking. And His way says that He loves us completely and unconditionally. It pleases Him greatly when we do things for Him and for the Kingdom, but He doesn't love us more when we do than when we don't. When we come to terms with that fact, it's very freeing, indeed.

This was the whole point behind the parable that Jesus shared with Simon and his friends who were there at his house on that occasion. The message also rings true for all of us who read it today. Authentic love for God leads us to realize and confess our sins, and this begins with acknowledging Jesus Christ as our Savior who forgives our sins. Then, our love moves us to actions of gratitude. Our deep gratitude intensifies our love, and our love increases our gratitude. And so it continues in one beautiful, ongoing circle!

Today's Touchpoint

Since it's so easy for us women to live life in the "seeking approval" mindset, we're going to close our day with a little practice in seeing ourselves as the handiwork of God.

List three positive qualities about yourself. Remember that you are God's *handiwork*. You are not bragging on yourself but on God.

1.

2.

3.

Talk to your heavenly Father about these characteristics. Ask Him to show you ways to use His design of you to bring Him glory.

Next, we all need encouragement from others. It sure feels good when we know we are appreciated and valued, doesn't it? As you think through the content of this week's study, ask the Holy Spirit to bring to mind someone who could use a good word to spur her on. Maybe it is someone who feels judged, someone who keeps to herself, or one who continually strives to please. Make contact with that person through a phone call or handwritten note. And when you do, be sure that you do it because you love God, not to win His approval.

Dear heavenly Father, my heart overflows with thanksgiving that You love me—no strings attached. Help me to remember this fact every time I start trying to earn Your approval by doing things for You. Help me to love You deeply so that everything I do is prompted by extravagant love and gratitude. Touch the heart of the person I plan to reach out to so that she may realize how much You love her. May I bring You pleasure with my offerings. I love You. Amen.

Day 5: Knowing Jesus Changes Everything

Focus: Moving Beyond Broken Dreams

Scripture:

⁴⁹And those who sat at the table with Him began to say to themselves, "Who is this who even forgives sins?"

⁵⁰Then He said to the woman, "Your faith has saved you. Go in peace."

Luke 7:49-50

They just didn't get it, did they? Simon's guests seated at the table with Jesus seemed pretty irked about His pronouncement of forgiveness of sins. They totally lost sight of what had happened in their midst. There was no room for joy in their hearts over forgiveness of sins, because their hearts were full of criticism of the One who'd forgiven the sins. They got sidetracked by the issue of blasphemy. In His claim of forgiving sin, Jesus also was claiming to be the Messiah. Since they did not believe this could possibly be true, they focused on the idea that He was a blasphemer of the Holy God of Israel.

And then something very beautiful happened. Jesus ignored them. Let's linger here a moment. He knew what was on their minds. There was plenty He could have said to them. But in that moment *she* was His priority. She stood before Him in humility and devotion—perhaps longing for His affirmation.

It saddens me to think of times when I've been caught up in issues rather than focusing on the people who needed attention. There will always be opportunities to engage in verbal sparring and debate over a variety of issues. But there are times when it would do much for the cause of Christ to simply follow His example and ignore the issues.

Is there a situation that comes to mind in which you now feel prompted to follow the example of Jesus and simply ignore an issue so that you can focus on a relationship?

Jesus lovingly turned His attention to her, addressing this one who had doused Him with "liquid passion." He affirmed her by letting her know that her sins had certainly been forgiven and she could now live in peace. In fact, He specifically gave her this directive: "Go in peace" (Luke 7:50).

Take a look at Jesus' words found in John 16:33 and write them below:

The Greek translation of the word Jesus used for *peace* in both Luke 7:50 and John 16:33 is *eiréné*, which means "peace of mind" or "wholeness."[4]

Where did Jesus say we would find this peace?

What did Jesus say we would have in the world?

In your own words, how would you describe what we experience while living here on earth?

As followers of Jesus, what reason do we have to "be of good cheer" (NKJV) or "be encouraged" (CEB)? How does this relate to Jesus' words about peace?

These words were spoken by a man who soon would be crucified. Yes, He was fully God, but He also was fully man. He knew that victory was certain in the face of every obstacle and challenge before Him. He knew the peace of living life with His Father. That same overcoming peace is possible for each and every child of God facing the challenges of life today. There are as many heartbreaking situations as there are people in the world.

Take a look at the list below. Circle those situations that have affected you or loved ones.

divorce	broken dreams	job loss	loss of privacy
health issues	serious illness	house fire	death of loved one
betrayal	deception	addiction	verbal/physical abuse
bankruptcy	theft	depression	family/relationship conflict

Are there others you'd like to add?

My friend, I feel such pain and inadequacy even putting words to these heartaches. Verbiage could never cover the pangs of grief and sheer agony that stab at us during our days of walking on earth. There are simply no words to describe the kind of physical, emotional, and mental torment that many of God's children face. But Jesus knows, and that's our comfort.

That short sentence containing only three words—"Go in peace"—was backed by all the power of the universe. I believe that when she heard Jesus' words, she realized that along with every sin He also knew every broken dream that had shattered her life. Surely she had dreams, just as we do.

I always dreamed of having the house in the neighborhood with the well-manicured lawn and white picket fence and kids playing in the front yard. I would be the neighbor who always showed up when you needed me, volunteered for school field trips, and had a husband who loved me—the perfect life. And then one day I awoke to my reality: a single mom struggling to buy diapers. I want to tell you that my faith never wavered and I handled it with ease. But the truth is, I struggled, sometimes moment to moment, to believe that the God who gave me those precious gifts would allow them to be taken away in the blink of an eye. At times I still wrestle with that.

~Anonymous

Maybe you join the ranks of many whose dreams of happiness never came true. Or maybe those dreams did spring forth for a while but shortly vaporized into a thick smog of disappointment, disillusionment, and heartache. So often that seems to be how life goes here on planet earth, doesn't it? Almost makes you cynical, you know—waiting for the other shoe to drop or the next bad thing to happen or your peace to be shattered once again.

It's no wonder we get dragged down. We live in a world tainted with sin. According to Matthew 5:45, it rains on the just and the unjust. Cancer is real and bad things happen to good people everywhere. The reality about dreams in life is that they don't always come true. If you have a broken dream, it may be the result of a marriage gone bad or the inability to pursue your vocation. Maybe you've had a miscarriage or suffered the death of a close friend or family member. The variety of broken dreams is great.

If you've ever faced this kind of heartache, briefly describe how it affected you.

Sometimes broken dreams result from situations and events beyond our control, and other times they are the result of our own bad choices and sin. As we've discussed, there is always forgiveness for our sin, but I feel the need to address those times when there are heartbreaking consequences as a result of our sin. The reality is that the *effects* of sin linger on this earth even when those sins have been forgiven and forgotten by God. As long as we are living with our memories intact, those effects of sin have the potential to take us under. It takes God living and moving within us to restore, heal, forgive, and move us forward.

Look at a portion of a letter I received from a woman who chose forgiveness over cynicism concerning her broken dreams. Worldly advice told her to leave her husband who had been unfaithful to her, but God showed her another way that was right for her situation.

Forgiveness is not an option but a commandment from our Lord. He tells us that He forgives us as we forgive others. When our heart beats in sync with His, forgiveness flows out of us as natural as breathing…. It all boils down to having the heart and desires of Jesus. He gives us the grace and forgiveness we need for our individual situations.

~ Anonymous

Would you agree with me that this incredible ability to forgive is only found by having the heart of Jesus Christ? Read again that last sentence of hers: "*He gives us the grace and forgiveness we need for our individual situations.*" We must remember that although forgiveness is a requirement rather than an option, biblically speaking, we do have options of how to deal with our individual circumstances. There are no formulas assigned to us. Our friend said it well: "It all boils down to having the heart and desires of Jesus."

My precious sister, your heavenly Father is here to comfort and guide you in the decisions He wants you to make regarding your particular broken dreams. He alone can tell you the steps to take. Rather than trying to determine what you think is right or wrong, ask yourself, "What does God say?"

Describe a situation (personal or otherwise) where it was evident that God was at work in the midst of broken dreams:

Using a print or online concordance, find a relevant Scripture that provides comfort for the heartaches of life and write it below.

We've spent an entire week with this nameless woman from Luke 7 who sought out the Lord for the sole purpose of expressing her love. When she steps onto the pages of Scripture, we are told she is a sinner, but we come to see her as she truly is in the heart of God: a regenerated, forgiven, whole woman. As I've mentioned, I imagine she had broken dreams just as we do. Surely as a young girl she did not dream of becoming a prostitute one day. Perhaps she shared the dreams of many little girls—dreams of having a husband who would love and cherish her. Surely she dreamed of living a life that would bring her fulfillment and purpose. And so, as I write these words, my heart leaps with joy over the love, acceptance, and purpose she discovered in Jesus Christ!

The same is true for us, dear friend; every broken dream you and I have ever experienced in this life is consummated—completed or perfected—in our union with Jesus Christ. Oh, how our very lives should move in praise with every breath we take. What *joy* is ours in Jesus!

Today's Touchpoint

What a love story we've explored this week. When this unnamed woman met Jesus, she met Hope. She went from a nobody judged by others to a somebody validated in the heart of God. Hope gave birth to freedom from sin's bondage, and freedom produced thanksgiving. Her deep thankfulness carried her broken spirit straight into the presence of the Lord! Her past was still a part of who she was, but it no longer *defined* who she was. Because of grace, she was able to push through her negative circumstances and emotions to discover new life in Jesus Christ!

Stepping in and out of Scripture quickly, this woman leaves us with a beautiful illustration of how God's grace can turn a life of fractured dreams into one of joyful and meaningful living.

Read Psalm 51:17 below—this week's memory verse. (You may want to look it up in several translations.) How does it relate to the story of the woman who anointed Jesus?

How does it relate to you—either currently or previously in your life?

How did God speak to your heart today?

Write Psalm 51:17 on an index card or a note in your phone or tablet and carry it with you today. Let God's word minister to your spirit. Also, be mindful of God's prompting to share this written message with someone He places before you. There have been many times He has prompted me to carry a Scripture in my pocket, leading me later to share it with another who is in need. If that opportunity should arise, take time later to write about your experience in your journal. May you be blessed as you minister to others in Jesus' name.

The sacrifices of God are a broken spirit,
A broken and a contrite heart—
These, O God, You will not despise. (Psalm 51:17)

Dear heavenly Father, I praise You for being Lord of my life and for ministering to me during times of brokenness. This dear woman in Scripture has been such an example to me of how to love You more deeply. Thank You that all our dreams are now fulfilled in You. What a joy it will be to meet her one day. But the greatest joy will be coming face to face with You! Amen.

● ● ● ● ● ●

Week 2
Video Viewer Guide

• •

Then one of the Pharisees asked Him to eat with him. And He went to the Pharisee's house, and sat down to eat. And behold, a woman in the city who was a sinner, when she knew that Jesus sat at the table in the Pharisee's house, brought an alabaster flask of fragrant oil.

Luke 7:36-37 NKJV

Relationship 1: Simon the Pharisee and Jesus

Simon was not a _____.

We become that woman on a mission to do things _____ God . . .

It's good until we let those good, wonderful things bypass the love _____.

Relationship 2: Jesus and the woman

She flat out _____ Jesus.

We find God in such _____ places.

She saved the time of _____ about what other people think.

Within love there is a newfound _____.

Week 2
Video Viewer Guide

Relationship 3: Jesus and you

He doesn't _____ our love, but He _____ us to give it to Him.

I want to encourage you to not let your devotional time get in the

way of your _____.

A _____ spirit is my sacrifice, God.

You won't despise a heart, God, that is broken and crushed.

Psalm 51:17 CEB

Week 3

The Woman with the Issue of Blood

When You Are Tired of Hurting

Her Story

²⁵Now a certain woman had a flow of blood for twelve years, ²⁶ and had suffered many things from many physicians. She had spent all that she had and was no better, but rather grew worse. ²⁷ When she heard about Jesus, she came behind Him in the crowd and touched His garment. ²⁸ For she said, "If only I may touch His clothes, I shall be made well."

²⁹ Immediately the fountain of her blood was dried up, and she felt in her body that she was healed of the affliction. ³⁰ And Jesus, immediately knowing in Himself that power had gone out of Him, turned around in the crowd and said, "Who touched My clothes?"

³¹ But His disciples said to Him, "You see the multitude thronging You, and You say, 'Who touched Me?'"

³² And He looked around to see her who had done this thing. ³³ But the woman, fearing and trembling, knowing what had happened to her, came and fell down before Him and told Him the whole truth. ³⁴ And He said to her, "Daughter, your faith has made you well. Go in peace, and be healed of your affliction."

Mark 5:25-34

Her Name: *Hurting*

As I think about this poor woman and her seemingly endless search for healing, I'm so grateful that her story is included in God's Word! There are many who are living with unbearable suffering today—perhaps you. If not you, then maybe someone close to you is hurting to the degree that life has been stripped of all joy. When affliction runs that deep, it takes every ounce of energy to make it through one day and get to the next. Whether it's physical, emotional, or mental, suffering takes a tremendous toll on the one going through it. And for those walking alongside those who suffer, the heartache runs deep.

However, there's great news for us in the midst of even the deepest affliction. The woman we read about in Mark 5 is nameless to us but known by God. He not only knew her name but He knew all about her suffering and her raw hurt. She reached for Him, and He tenderly turned her way.

Just as our Lord met her needs, so He longs to meet the needs of all who live with suffering today. Thankfully, this woman's story does not end in her anguish but in her healing! What is true for this woman whose companion was continual misery is true for all believers in the Great Physician: God is able and willing to heal!

Dear friend, my heart is excited to climb into this week's study with you. I'm excited because there are many who have shared your "suffering stories" with me. I know from God's Word that He longs to strengthen you and help you in whatever trial you're trudging through. And from experience, I can attest to the reliability of God's compassion and healing of my soul during such convoluted seasons of my own life.

I've made it through some physical, emotional, and mental distresses that, at the time, seemed nearly unbearable to me. Clinical depression brought on by emotional and physical pain held me captive for years. Thankfully, I later experienced healing in those areas, but the greatest healing came before the physical healings occurred. It was a healing of my soul that came about as I handed the reins of my life over to my heavenly Father.

My mind often displays the still-frame of the moment my heart was regenerated. Taking a walk through our neighborhood, I was beyond functioning. With my emotions bottomed out and my body aching, I fell to my knees.

"Lord, I don't think it's Your will that I go crazy, but here I go—and I'm going for You!"

I can't describe how it happened, but somehow in that moment of mental, emotional, and physical anguish God manifested His healing within my spirit. Trust seemed to explode in my heart at that moment. For the first time during my struggle, I let go of trying to get better. I trusted Him with my whole life, even if it meant that I'd never recover. To state it simply, trusting God became my focus instead of being healed!

It's the very picture of Matthew 5:3 as stated in *The Message* Bible:

> *"You're blessed when you're at the end of your rope. With less of you there is more of God and his rule."*

God sometimes extends physical or circumstantial healings, but quite often there's a deeper healing that He has in mind. It's a healing of the heart where you learn to trust Him whether or not your physical or earthly condition changes. It involves getting rid of self and allowing God to reign as Lord of your life. That healing, my dear sister, is the grandest healing of all!

Memory Verse

"Fear not, for I am with you;
Be not dismayed, for I am your God.
I will strengthen you,
Yes, I will help you,
I will uphold you with My righteous right hand."

Isaiah 41:10

Each phrase of this verse is mighty! Your God is bound by His word to strengthen, help, and keep you from falling apart. I encourage you to memorize one phrase at a time as you talk to your heavenly Father about that part of His promise to you.

Day 1: Depleted And Done

Focus: Purpose in Suffering

Scripture:

[25]Now a certain woman had a flow of blood for twelve years, [26]and had suffered many things from many physicians. She had spent all she had and was no better, but rather grew worse.

Mark 5:25-26

I had been teaching school for several years when the pain started inching up my left jawline toward my ear. Months passed, and it seemed that nothing I did to alleviate the ache helped. Months turned into years, and I finally sought out a doctor to get some relief. What had been mild at first was now intense and had spread to both jaws and temples. X-rays were taken, and there seemed to be no physical reason I was hurting. I remember very well the mental and emotional exasperation I felt when the third doctor, who was a neurologist, told me, "There is no reason physiologically for your pain." It was year fifteen of suffering, and I was done!

Have you ever been in physical pain for so long that you wanted to give up? If so, briefly describe how you felt during this situation.

With me being pretty much debilitated, my husband took over the search for treatment and found a maxillofacial doctor for us to visit. A consultation along with X-rays of the jaw areas revealed that I was a sufferer of the temporomandibular joint disorder, otherwise known as TMJ. Now I was bona fide in my complaints. Hope returned in the midst of intense suffering with the knowledge that someone finally understood what I was going through and would pay attention to my pain. It just took the right doctor to diagnose the problem and set me on the road to healing.

This unnamed woman in Mark 5 and I have shared similar frustrations. Even though thousands of years separate our journeys, there's a common thread in the adversity we both experienced.

- Her pain lasted for many years; so did mine.
- She invested much financially; so did I.

- She had many doctor visits with no remedy for pain; same with me.
- Instead of getting better, she only got worse; same here.

Do you see the connection? I'm confident that this story written long ago is intended to give hope and encouragement to everyone reading it today! God's Word confirms this very thing:

> *For the word of God is living and powerful, and sharper than any two-edged sword, piercing even to the division of soul and spirit, and of joints and marrow, and is a discerner of the thoughts and intents of the heart.*
>
> Hebrews 4:12

Yes, living and powerful is His Word. While the Bible was completed approximately two millenia ago, its authority and application for us today remain unchanged. It continues to be the sole authority of the revelation God has given us about Himself and His plan for humanity. Our living and present-tense Bible is the holy description of who God is and what He desires for each individual He created. His Word is never out of date, nor can it be improved. Yes, cultures have changed and generations have come and gone, but the Word of God is as relevant to you and me as it was when it was first written, my friend.

So, let's explore what the Bible says about pain and suffering and apply it to our lives today. The Scripture that got me through my worst days is found in 2 Corinthians:

> *But we have this treasure in earthen vessels, that the excellence of the power may be of God and not of us. We are hard-pressed on every side, yet not crushed; we are perplexed, but not in despair; persecuted, but not forsaken; struck down, but not destroyed—always carrying about in the body the dying of the Lord Jesus, that the life of Jesus also may be manifested in our body.*
>
> 2 Corinthians 4:7-10

What does "treasure in earthen vessels" mean to you?

I sometimes have difficulty remembering that there's treasure in this earthly vessel of mine. That's especially true if I'm suffering in some way. Feeling cruddy keeps me distracted from Who is living on the inside. Listen, my friend. If Jesus Christ has taken up residence in your life, then He doesn't depart when things go terribly wrong in your body or mind (thank You, Lord!). Perhaps it will help us better remember this truth if we take a deeper look at Paul's words.

According to the Greek meaning of the phrase "treasure in earthen vessels," our bodies are actually a storehouse where good and precious things are laid up. Think of it: as believers, our bodies hold Christ Himself and His treasures. Doesn't that knowledge make you view yourself a tad differently when you look in the mirror?

Imagine with me for a moment. What do you think some of these treasures might be?

The Scripture goes on to report that the reason we house this wonderful treasure is so that "the excellence of the power may be of God and not of us" (v. 7). In other words, this is a power for performing miracles—a power that is only possible and permissible by God Himself!

I've been in that place, haven't you? I'm talking about moments when there was absolutely nothing left of my physical, mental, and emotional resources to deal with what was facing me. I was spent, exhausted, and depleted—you know, totally worn out and ready to give up. It was during some of those "weakened but mighty" moments that God displayed His Glory in a powerful way. I knew as well as others around me that there was no Cindi operating then; there was only God's mightiness at work!

In those times it's the Matthew 5:3 principle at work:

> *"You're blessed when you're at the end of your rope. With less of you there is more of God and his rule." (The Message)*

There's a powerful supernatural principle at work in holy submission.

Using a print or online dictionary, define the two words below:

submission

resignation

How is submitting different from resigning?

Which one is honoring to God, and why?

Now take a look at 2 Corinthians 12:10 and write the verse below:

What is Paul doing for Christ's sake?

Where do you tend to fall on the "delighting" in suffering scale? Make an X on the line below.

1	5	10
(not at all)	(need some work)	(bring it on)

Look what else Paul says about our suffering in the Book of Romans:

> *I consider that our present sufferings are not worth comparing with the glory that will be revealed in us.*

Romans 8:18 NIV

I clearly remember the moment years ago when this verse took hold of me. I was mulling over Scripture and contemplating my "suffering" while I was working through household chores one day. All of a sudden it was as if the Holy Spirit simply interpreted that verse, speaking directly to me. (That's His role, you know.) Here's what I sensed Him saying in that instant: *The intensity of your suffering will one day be far surpassed by the intensity of My glory!*

For me at that moment, that message from above was shouting ground! There was a lot of physical and emotional suffering surrounding me, and that translated to *a lot of glory* headed my way.

Is this a promise you can hold onto, my friend? Do you think you could possibly train yourself to think about *glory revealed* more often than you think about your *present suffering*?

Here's another verse to give you aid in your training regimen:

For our light and momentary troubles are achieving for us an eternal glory that far outweighs them all.

2 Corinthians 4:17 NIV

Think about your current situation or a previous struggle you have had. In your own words, state what the truth as recorded in these two Scriptures means for you personally:

As I ponder the Scriptures in our study today, I'm setting some personal goals. Check the goals below you'd like to set for yourself. Add another, if you'd like.

__I want to be continually mindful of the treasure living inside of me.
__I want to allow God to explode His glory through my suffering.
__I want to become less preoccupied with my pain and more preoccupied with His power.
__I want to learn how to delight in my weaknesses and afflictions.
__I want to live in the reality of one day experiencing His glory after my suffering ends.
__ Other:_____

Now, go back and review 2 Corinthians 4:7-10. List below the reality of life in Christ as Paul describes it. I've done the first one for you.

hard-pressed on every side, yet not crushed

perplexed, but _____

persecuted, but _____

struck down, but _____

Not crushed, not in despair, not forsaken, and *not destroyed.* This is not only wonderful news; it's *true* news! This is our reality because of the treasure living inside of us. And why? So that the "life of Jesus also may be manifested in our body" and, I would add, in our circumstances.

Okay, a little word study here. Using a print or online dictionary, look up the word *manifest*. What does it mean when used as a verb?

Paul uses the phrase "may be manifested in our body" to teach us that because of the work of Christ Who lives inside of us, we have the opportunity to use our sufferings to make the glory of Christ known. Oh my, how I long to store up this word in my heart and apply it when the suffering hits!

Sister, read these words again with new understanding:

> *Now a certain woman had a flow of blood for twelve years, and had suffered many things from many physicians. She had spent all she had and was no better, but rather grew worse.*
>
> Mark 5:25-26

This nameless woman known to us as "the woman with the issue of blood" has impacted the lives of countless people throughout the years. I've named her *Hurting* for our study. I knew we were sisters when I read the first couple of sentences of her story. Many years and different cultures separate us, but we share the same heavenly Father. The reality that she suffered for so long but only grew worse as she searched for a cure actually gives us hope. Why? Because we know the rest and the best of her story—Jesus!

Today's Touchpoint

Using a concordance or perhaps a key-word search from an online Bible dictionary, look up the word *suffering*. Record three verses that seem to apply directly to current or previous suffering that you or a loved one may have experienced.

1.

2.

3.

Trials and sufferings can be a great door-opener to sharing the love of Jesus Christ. We don't have to look very far to find someone who is miserable because of circumstances she or he is going through. This pain may be physical or emotional. The effects of *any* type of suffering can be very detrimental and cause great discouragement on top of the pain that is already being endured.

Ask your heavenly Father to place on your heart right now someone who is going through hardship. Now ask Him to show you some ways you might encourage that person. List some possibilities below.

Pray over these ideas and then choose one and reach out to this person sometime this week. Return here later to write about your experience in the space below, or record your reflections in a journal:

Dear heavenly Father, I confess to You that it's difficult for me to thank You for pain and suffering in my life. When I'm hurting, it's often difficult to see You and Your purpose in my suffering. By faith, I simply say "thank You" for what You are teaching me through such difficult trials. I pray, dear Father, that You will remind me that You are my strength and my helper. Help me to show Your compassion to others who are hurting. I love You. Amen.

Day 2: Desperate For Jesus

Focus: Not Giving Up

Scripture:

27When she heard about Jesus, she came behind Him in the crowd and touched His garment. 28For she said, "If only I may touch His clothes, I shall be made well."

Mark 5:27-28

Overall, I'm a positive person. I've found that I can often pep myself up and entirely change my outlook on the day by thinking and speaking positive words. But sometimes, the point is better caught by speaking in negative tones. That's why I've selected the focus for this day to be *not giving up*, as opposed to *keep on trying*.

Listen: If you are at rock bottom, an all-time low, and living in the pits, hear my shout: *Don't you dare give up*!

As we continue to journey with the woman who was depleted and done with it all, I want you to catch that something in her spirit that drove her on. Yes, there was a smidgen of a smidgen that kept her from throwing in the towel. Personally, I believe that "something" was the Spirit of our Lord Himself. I believe He was drawing her so that He could be glorified in her life at that moment, as well as for years to come. And based on the Scriptures, including the one below, I believe He is drawing you and thinking about you as you contemplate His intervention during your times of suffering.

> *Your eyes saw me when I was formless;*
> *all my days were written in Your book and planned*
> *before a single one of them began.*
> Psalm 139:16 HCSB

Let's park here just for a moment to take in the awesome reality of this verse. How does your heart respond to the truth that God knew all about your life before you were even formed?

The Greek word for "written" in this verse is *kathab*. It's the same word used in Exodus 31:18 detailing how Moses was given "two tablets of stone, written with the finger of God."[1] God knows you to the depths of your being. He knows you better than you know yourself. The details of your life—now and yet to come—are recorded in His heart, written by His finger. And according to His Word, not one moment of angst has gone unnoticed:

> *You've kept track of my every toss and turn*
> *through the sleepless nights,*
> *Each tear entered in your ledger,*
> *each ache written in your book.*
> Psalm 56:8 *The Message*

As we suffer, God is not absent. He is there in the suffering with us, waiting and watching and longing to ease our pain. As you are reading these words, the sovereign God of our universe has *you* on His mind. Your story is written out in His book. When suffering enters in, it's not lost in some kind of mayhem of stress. He knows about every second of your every day, and He cares! He is always drawing you and giving you opportunities to reach out for Him. And sometimes those opportunities come blaring when you go through a time of ongoing suffering.

Do you recall a time that God drew you to Himself through suffering? If so, briefly describe it below:

Do you remember the meaning of Immanuel, Christ's name? You can find it in Matthew 1:23 if you've forgotten. Immanuel means:

What is one reason it is critical to remember that He is always with us?

As I think through our Scripture passage for the week, I'm reminded that this woman named *Hurting* had a choice. Although I personally believe Jesus was drawing her to Himself, I also believe He gave her the choice to respond by reaching out to Him. Jesus never forces anyone to seek and receive what He has to offer. He simply provides the opportunity to do so. This woman was certainly at a crossroads in her life, positioned at a juncture that demanded a response on her part.

juncture – a point of time; especially: one made critical by a concurrence of circumstances[2]

Yes, indeed; it was a critical moment involving a choice that would determine the quality of the rest of her living days. Would she hang it all up, finally giving in to her depths of despair? Or would she latch on to that faint hope that maybe this was the One who could and would heal her?

Of course, we're privy to how it all went down, and we have celebrated the results of her choice. She didn't know this side of heaven how this single decision to go after Jesus would offer hope and encouragement to countless hurting people.

In view of her story, I have three other suffering women from life today on my heart.

Two Friends and an Anonymous Woman

Last night I tossed and turned throughout the night, full of concern for a friend who is deeply hurting. Circumstances of life have positioned her in such a place that she's now at a crossroads. She has no power over her circumstances, but she does have the power of choice. She can choose to believe that God is in control and that He has not left her in a prison of physical, mental, and emotional debris.

The night before last, I was troubled throughout the night because of the deep suffering of another friend. Her mind and emotions seem totally paralyzed because of negative circumstances. Those issues have landed her in the pit of despair. She has the same choice as my first friend. She can choose to believe that God is in control and has a plan for her life, even at this moment, or she can spiral forever downward, letting her misery overtake her.

What is similar with my two friends is this: both have been knocked off balance by circumstances that are beyond their control. But there's a contrast, and herein lies the difference in their individual responses. One has an abiding relationship with Jesus Christ. The other does not. The choice to believe in and follow Jesus can alter every seemingly hopeless situation that could possibly confront us! I like the hope of 2 Corinthians 4:8-9. We read these verses yesterday, but look at the wording from the Common English Bible:

> *We are experiencing all kinds of trouble, but we aren't crushed. We are confused, but we aren't depressed. We are harassed, but we aren't abandoned. We are knocked down, but we aren't knocked out.*

While it's true that both my friends are suffering beyond what I can imagine, one is hanging on to hope based on her relationship with Jesus Christ; the other is not. They're both knocked down, but the one who knows Jesus, although knocked down for the moment, is not knocked out!

Now take a peek at an anonymous woman whose circumstances could have easily left her feeling hopeless. Here's a portion of the letter I received from her:

I have been struggling with physical pain and a whole lot of emotional pain. I was diagnosed with lupus and fibromyalgia in recent years. It has been a daily struggle for me. It is hard to cope with. I have three children and a husband. Some days all I want to do is sleep. That sums up the physical pain…now on to the emotional pain…

Can't you just feel her heart in this brief sharing? I wanted to hug her and cry along with her as I continued reading her story…

During a period of about two years we had lost twelve very close relatives, which made my struggle with God even harder. My thoughts were, "Hasn't our family been through enough? How much more pain must we encounter before God gives us a break?" For about two and a half years I was in a state of numbness, confusion. . . .I was heartbroken. Those days are kind of a blur to me. I managed to make it through, though.

Read those words again: *I managed to make it through, though.* Yes, somewhere in her state of numbness, confusion, and heartbreak, she mustered up enough energy *not* to call it quits. How? Because she knew God was with her. She ended with this:

I do know that with God's guidance I will get through this. Even through the pain, I know God has a plan.

~Anonymous

My friends, sometimes the only energy you have left is the energy to not give up. If that's true for you right now, then hang on to that holy morsel of hope.

That's the amount of energy it took for the woman with the issue of blood to reach one tired and weary hand toward Jesus. And that's the amount of energy it takes for *you* to do the same.

For years as I struggled with pain and depression, I latched onto this promise:

Now thanks be *to God who always leads us in triumph in Christ.*
2 Corinthians 2:14a

Focusing there kept me steady and rock-solid as I based my outlook on the truth of Scripture instead of on my feelings. In my Bible beside that verse I wrote these words: "Whether it looks like it or not!"

Reaching toward Jesus with even a trace of hope will set you on the road to victory. God may or may not change your circumstances. And if He does, it may take longer than you imagined it would take. But if you turn to Him, He will fill your heart with His presence, and that will be more than enough to get you through.

Today's Touchpoint

We will continue exploring this topic over the next several days. For today, I want you to be proactive in dealing with a particular painful issue that involves you or someone you know. There have been seasons of my life when I was the one touched with affliction and heartache. During other times, I've been the one commissioned by the Spirit to reach out to one who is hurting.

Referring to my description, circle the phrase that best describes you today:

touched with affliction   commissioned to reach out to the hurting

If you are going through a season of hurt, there is someone who would love to pray with you and share your heartache. However, if you're like most people, the angst of letting someone know you're in need is right up there with jumping out of a three-story window. Let me encourage you by reminding you that letting someone know your need and asking her to walk alongside you would be allowing another to experience a blessing. God gave us friends who will share our burdens, and each time we do so, we give others the opportunity to love us as Christ loves us. Loving as He loves always blesses us.

Make the effort to share your burden with someone today. As you have time, record your feelings about your experience below or in a journal:

Or, if the Holy Spirit is prompting you to reach out to someone else with the love of Jesus, then make a deliberate effort to connect with someone you know who is hurting. This may or may not be the person who came to mind yesterday.

Go beyond writing a note or making a phone call. Schedule a time when you can meet her for a walk or coffee, or invite her over for a chat. As time permits, write about your experience below or in a journal.

My friend, as we close today's study time together, may you continue to draw strength from God's Word to face whatever suffering is before you now or whatever suffering you may face later—for we know that if this very moment doesn't hold a storm, then one could pop up at any moment. I'm not being pessimistic; remember, I'm a *positive* thinker. I'm merely stating a biblical fact. Jesus said,

> *"These things I have spoken to you, that in Me you may have peace. In the world you will have tribulation; but be of good cheer, I have overcome the world."*
>
> John 16:33

Remember, my friend, we always have reason to be of good cheer. Jesus has overcome the world and *all* our suffering!

Dear heavenly Father, thank You that You never gave up on me even when I gave up on myself. I'm so grateful that Your love draws me into Your saving grace. Right now I especially thank You for the journey of this suffering woman we read about in Mark 5. Her story and Your healing inspire me to turn my "desperate" into "desperate for You." Give me a tender heart just like Yours so that I am sensitive to reach out to those around me who suffer. In the healing name of Jesus I pray. Amen.

Day 3: Healed by Jesus

Focus: Recognizing and Receiving God's Healing

Scripture:

[29]Immediately her bleeding stopped and she felt in her body that she was freed from her suffering. [30]At once Jesus realized that power had gone out from him. He turned around in the crowd and asked, "Who touched my clothes?"

Mark 5:29-30 NIV

I still remember the moment I awoke from my TMJ surgery. Even in the grogginess of those first few minutes, I remember being ecstatic over being out of pain. The moments during the ride to the hospital had been filled with tears of agony from the intense hurt pounding in both jaws. Yep, I was one happy chick to be freed from suffering. Even though barely awake, my soul was giving high-fives and turning cartwheels of joy!

If you've ever experienced being *freed* from suffering, briefly describe how you felt:

I wonder how our Mark 5 friend *Hurting* felt as she was suddenly released from her pain. I'm seeing her in a new way now.

I've been fascinated by getting to know these anonymous women from Scripture. Their individual stories intrigue me. I've enjoyed researching their cultures and lifestyles. The better I get to know them, the more curious I become about how they interacted with Jesus. For each one, I imagine what happened during that holy moment when she and Jesus came together face to face and heart to heart. Was there an explosion of joy, or was it more of a subtle encounter? Did she sense a whisper of promise to her soul? And with our story this week, I wonder if her world rocked with joy and excitement over *fresh healing*, just as mine did when I awoke from surgery.

Think about what took place in the heart and mind of this dear woman who lived in anguish for twelve long years. Let your imagination roll, and describe below how she possibly felt at the moment she realized she was healed.

This phrase from one of the psalms comes to mind when I think of being delivered from physical, emotional, or mental pain:

> *Weeping may spend the night,*
> *but there is joy in the morning.*
> Psalm 30:5 HCSB

My friend, it's true that we will all face trials during our lives. Here's the wonderful news: if you are in relationship with Jesus Christ, your suffering will always be followed by peace and restoration—if not immediately, then eventually.

I often thought of the woman with the issue of blood last year as I sat in a zero gravity chair, wishing the pain from my herniated disc would go away. I felt useless. I had never been in this kind of pain before. I've always known that God loves me, and our relationship has always been sweet. However, being in chronic pain changes everything! I couldn't pray. I didn't pick up my Bible for over a month. I couldn't do anything without hurting. Where was the light at the end of the tunnel? I kept thinking about the woman with the issue of blood. Twelve years? What a long, dark tunnel she must have experienced. But oh, how sweet when the Master came along! There's nothing, absolutely nothing, like walking out of that dark tunnel into His glorious light. I am so thankful that the Great Physician is still in the healing business.

~ Anonymous

Yes, He's definitely still in the healing business! I've come to discover, however, that God's healings don't always come with such pomp and circumstance. Sometimes the healing process He uses seems excruciatingly long. And there are other times when we realize the healing we long for is not to be realized here but is waiting on us when we move our residency to heaven.

So far we've explored those healings that occurred quite dramatically after long bouts with pain. If I had to guess, I'd say that most of you reading these words would jump at the chance for you or someone you love to be added to the list of those who've experienced that dramatic kind of healing, right? But most of the healings we experience are more of the lackluster variety, it seems. Suffering, for many, lasts for a very long time. That's why these words of Jesus are particularly comforting, and they bear repeating:

> *"You will have suffering in this world. Be courageous! I have conquered the world."*
>
> John 16:33b HCSB

The Greek word for *suffering* in this verse, *thlipsis*, is one that means a "pressing together" or "pressure."[3]

My heart is sad thinking about how our Lord must have felt this pressure of burdens just before His death.

Turn to Matthew 26:39. Write it below:

In His humanity, how might Jesus have felt this pressure of burdens? Write your thoughts below.

Now write a phrase or two to describe how you've felt this pressure of burdens in the following areas:

Mental:

Emotional:

Taking the words of Jesus in John 16:33 to heart, what do you think His intention is for you in your suffering?

If I loaned my journals to you, you could read my ramblings written en route to the recoveries I've experienced. Some of these healings were physical; some were emotional and mental. You'd find that on occasion I failed to recognize God's instruments of healing He placed before me. To me they seemed unlikely tools for Him to use. That was the case during my clinical-depression years. Always a strong Christian, I believed I could pray my way out of any negative circumstance. Being attacked by this monster of an illness was no different for me. I would just commit to praying long and hard enough, and it would go away—or so I thought.

Weeks rolled over into months, and the months gave way to years. Finally, the only thing left to do outside of praying was to visit my doctor. His words rang true: "When you've been under continual stress for a long period of time, the chemicals in your brain get out of whack, and it's necessary to use medicine to get them back in line." What followed was a pretty nasty argument: me with me. I seemed unable to recognize and receive the truth that antidepressants would be a tool God would use to set me on the road to recovery. This was the early nineties, and I'd heard teaching from the Christian community that Christians were not placing enough faith in God if they were using medicine to overcome depression.

What are your feelings about God using medicine to bring you or someone else through clinical depression?

On what do you base these feelings?

I look back on those days now and can hardly believe it took me so long to visit my doctor. By the time I got to him, I'd had many experiences of *sitting on the floor and wondering how I would get up and go into the next room.* My friend! If you are at this place of non-functioning, and if you know it's more than a case of the blues you're experiencing, you need to seek medical attention. I encourage you to visit a trusted healthcare provider and follow the treatment program prescribed. I'm so thankful I did! I can also tell you that I know God led me to this kind doctor who used medicine that God created through human beings as part of His plan to restore my health. (If you are in need of more guidance and prayer over this topic, please click the prayer link on the homepage of my website, www.frazzledfemale.com. Our prayer team will help point you in the direction you need.)

Finally, during my illness, I recognized and received the healing provided by God. Much like the Mark 5 woman, though not in the same way, I'd suffered deeply. My desperation was the holy vehicle used by God to recognize and receive the healing treatment He designed for me.

Are you open to God's plan for healing in your life? Are you willing to receive His power in whatever way He chooses to give it? Are you willing to lay down self-effort and false pretenses, thus revealing your vulnerabilities before others? For me, there was a lot of pride stored up through years of being the "go-to" person for prayer and spiritual insight. It was extremely difficult for me to allow my suffering to be exposed to my friends—and even to my family. Blasting through those areas of pride, however, ushered me into God's healing.

Share in a couple of sentences about what God is revealing to your heart right now concerning this area of suffering.

Jesus knew what had occurred at the moment the hemorrhaging woman was healed. He knew the healing properties that were transferred from His body into hers. He knew who had touched Him, because He knows all things. And yet He asked, "Who touched My clothes?" (Mark 5:30).

I get a charge out of this question. The disciples' reaction makes me giggle: "You see the multitude thronging You, and You say, 'Who touched Me?'" (Mark 5:31).

I sense new facets of God's personality as I get to know my Lord on deeper levels. Can't you see the humor right here? Remembering how Jesus loved interacting with others helps me to stay engaged with Him in a fresh and lively way. I can imagine He was waiting for this teachable moment and truly enjoyed playing it out—just my thinking.

Why do you think Jesus would ask such a question? List some possibilities below.

Jesus turned around as He asked the question, looking at the woman. I imagine He scanned the onlookers as He did, with a twinkle in His eye. During this moment, her cure was made known. The manifestation of His glory and the glory of God shone in those suspended moments of heightened anticipation and awe. And what a glorious moment it was!

Today's Touchpoint

Jesus was fully God. He was also fully man, with emotions and personality. The life of Christ on earth portrayed in the Scriptures reveals this, helping us to better relate to Him. It's true that life is full of pain and suffering. Everywhere you turn there are those hurting in some way. In fact, it's rare to have days that are totally free of some kind of suffering—whether your own or that of others. Physical and emotional pain saps your energy and can make you stale.

Let's close our time together by taking a "refresh" break! Let our imagined twinkle in Jesus' eye jumpstart you into energizing your relationship with Him. Sometime today, do something just for fun as you talk and listen to Him. This might be a leisurely walk or a short drive or even a nap. The goal is to take a little time just to enjoy hanging out with your Lord. Ask Him to give you fresh insight into His love. If you are suffering in some way right now, thank Him for His delivery to come. If you are not hurting, thank Him for this season of being free from pain.

Dear heavenly Father, You've told us that life here will be full of pain and suffering. Since I believe Your Word and live in this imperfect world, I believe that to be true. I confess, Lord, that it's so easy to stay hunkered down in pain. Hurting just makes me so self-focused. I need Your energy and outlook to give me fresh purpose in living. Help me right now to see Your smile and the twinkle in Your eye as You turn my way. I love You. Amen.

Day 4: Our Merciful Savior

Focus: His Cleansing Power

Scripture:

32And He looked around to see her who had done this thing. 33But the woman, fearing and trembling, knowing what had happened to her, came and fell down before Him and told Him the whole truth.

Mark 5:32-33

She knew that He was close by and would make His way through the crowd. She didn't know that He was waiting and ready to heal her. We learn from the Scriptures that she had heard about Jesus. I wonder if what she'd heard about Him was what gave her that tiny bit of hope that just maybe He could and would cure her from her infirmity. Maybe this thought had sparked in her mind after she'd heard how He had cured the many sick people who had been brought to Him. But perhaps as she remembered she was "unclean" and no one would want to help her get to Jesus, her hope may have wavered.

Then again, she'd likely heard how He had taught about forgiveness and seemed to be drawn to the sick, hurting, and shunned. He'd moved among the crowds with such kindness, especially to the afflicted and outcast. She was about as afflicted as they came, she may have reasoned. Everyone in and around town knew she was unclean, so she surely qualified as an outcast. Since He seemed drawn to this kind, perhaps He would be willing to heal her.

Dangling from a thread of desire, she inched her way toward the One she hoped would save her. She had become a woman on a mission; her sole objective was to reach out and touch the hem of the One who could free her from her suffering—and from herself.

Have you ever been a *woman on a mission* to experience something from the Lord? If so, describe your situation.

Read Hebrews 11:1. According to this definition, how does faith propel our actions?

Hurting had a particular reason in mind for this mission to touch the hem of the Lord's garment. So by faith she moved forward. Without studying the Bible, we could easily dismiss the *touching* of His robe as merely reaching for the most accessible part of His clothing. Scripture reveals something else, however. God gave specific instructions under the Mosaic law regarding the corners or fringes of the garments worn by His people.

> *The LORD said to Moses: Speak to the Israelites and say to them: Make fringes on the edges of your clothing for all time. Have them put blue cords on the fringe on the edges. This will be your fringe. You will see it and remember all the LORD's commands and do them. Then you won't go exploring the lusts of your own heart or your eyes. In this way you'll remember to do all my commands. Then you will be holy to your God. I am the LORD your God, who brought you out of the land of Egypt to be your God. I am the LORD your God.*
>
> Numbers 15:37-41 CEB

The corners of the robe reminded the people of their connection with God; they were symbolic of being identified with God.

Take a look at Ruth 3:9. What did Ruth ask Boaz to do?

Asking him to spread the corner of his garment over her was making a request of him to identify with her.

When Jesus lived on earth and people reached for the corners of His garment, it was surely a sign that they wanted to be identified with Him. That's because the Jewish people living in Jesus' day were familiar with the Hebrew Scriptures. They had been steeped in them during their growing up years. In fact, the Pharisees often were guilty of overkill in their show to be closely identified with God.

> *Everything they do, they do to be noticed by others. They make extra-wide prayer bands for their arms and long tassels for their clothes.*
>
> Matthew 23:5 CEB

Because devout Jewish men wore these "tassels of remembrance" on their robes, Jesus most likely wore them often. (And it goes without saying that His were not like the elaborate showpieces worn by the Pharisees.)

There were no healing elements in the clothes that Jesus wore. No. It was *faith* in Him that brought the healing.

● ● ● ● ● ●

Read Matthew 14:34-36 and Mark 6:56. What kind of people were brought to Jesus, and what were they begging to do?

Given the particulars surrounding this dear woman and her determination to get to Jesus, I offer my own personal conclusions:

1. Her point of desperation was what led her to Jesus. Stripped of pride and dignity, her faith kicked in and moved her through that crowd to get to the Lord.

2. She may have believed He was the Messiah, the Promised One from God. In any case, she believed He could heal her physically and circumstantially.

3. She knew that according to the law, she was unclean because of her blood. She also knew that according to the law, touching Jesus would render Him unclean.

4. She likely had heard Jesus preach about the good news of the kingdom of God and may have concluded that her touch would not affect His purity but would, rather, end her nightmare of suffering.

5. Her spirit was laced with holy fear and trembling as she acknowledged her boldness to the Lord about what she had done.

I believe it was this dear woman's combination of distress, hope, and faith that moved her forward. Her bold actions walked her right up to the heart of God. As Jesus turned to look at her and saw her fear and trembling, His mercy kicked in. Mercy is best described as *God's attitude toward those who are in distress.*

Why do you think she was fearful and trembling?

Using a print or online Bible dictionary, look up the word *distress*. Write several phrases that describe this woman based on the meanings you find.

Do any of these phrases describe *you*?

Just as Jesus turned to face this hurting woman, He turns to face you. He knew all about her affliction and hurting heart, just as He knows all about yours.

He knows that suffering is a holy instrument for shining His glory. He received much glory from this woman's suffering state and healing on that day. Perhaps as you understand how He was glorified in her suffering, you'll garner strength to allow Him to be glorified in yours.

Let's review the nature of her distress.

Her physical issue	Her hemorrhaging had caused great physical duress for twelve long years.
Her financial issue	Seeking help from the medical field during her extended illness depleted the money she had.
Her emotional issue	The reality of not getting better but growing worse—on top of dealing with depleted finances and ongoing bleeding—surely left her on the threshold of despair.
Her social issue	She was shunned by family, friends, and society; due to the nature of her illness, this was the law.

In order to understand the heart of this woman and the depth of her distress, it's necessary to take a look at the times in which she lived. The culture of the day, along with old covenant law, made her situation even more problematic. From our twenty-first century vantage point, we can relate to her physically, financially, and emotionally. It's more difficult, however, for us to understand what she was experiencing relationally. I could imagine that this separation from family and friends, along with being marked as a social outcast, was possibly the deepest of all the suffering. We've mentioned the fact that she would have been declared *unclean*, but let's take a deeper look at what that means.

Read Leviticus 15:19-33 and answer the following questions:

How long was a woman separated from others when she had her menstrual bleeding?

What happened to people who touched her or touched things she had touched?

After the bleeding stopped, how many days were there before she was pronounced clean?

What happened if the blood continued to flow?

Imagine with me for a moment what it must have been like living under those old covenant laws and regulations. Regarding the questions above, how would your life have been impacted so far?

According to the Mosaic law, a woman was unclean and an outcast all because her body was following its natural physical cycles. Being ceremonially unclean in this way prevented her from contact with anyone around her. If she was married or had children, she was separated from them. She was barred from worshipping God and being with God's people until she was made clean. She was isolated, much as one who had leprosy. She had to be purified to correct her unclean condition.

Dig deeply with me. Do you see any correlation here to how sin isolates and separates us from God?

Complete the following statements based on what you know to be true about your condition without the saving grace of Jesus. (Write the words of your choice.)

My _____ separates me from God.

The _____ of Christ is my only hope for _____.

My sister, as we close our study today, meditate on Christ's saving grace outlined in the verse below, and pause for a few moments to offer heartfelt thanks to Him for His blood that set us free from such constraints of the law.

However, we know that a person isn't made righteous by the works of the Law but rather through the faithfulness of Jesus Christ. We ourselves believed in Christ Jesus so that we could be made righteous by the faithfulness of Christ and not by the works of the Law—because no one will be made righteous by the works of the Law.

Galatians 2:16 CEB

Today's Touchpoint

It's often difficult to sense God's presence when you are suffering. Your body, mind, and emotions seem to become all wrapped up in self instead of God's loving presence surrounding you.

Why do you think this is true?

Turn to Psalm 34. Choose several verses to write in the space provided on the next page or in your journal, talking to the Lord about helping you to believe they are true for you. Here is one of my journal entries:

I will bless the Lord *at all times;*
His praise shall *continually* be *in my mouth.*
Psalm 34:1

Lord, I've often thought about how pain turns me inward. When I'm hurting, it's just hard to think about anything other than how terrible I feel. Please bring me out of my self-centeredness so that I can be a light to shine Your glory. Right now I choose to focus on praising and loving You regardless of how I feel. I love You and trust You to bring Yourself glory out of my suffering.

Your turn:

When you make a conscious effort to praise the Lord when you're suffering as well as when you're not, you're developing a discipline that takes root in your heart and mind. I'm no expert by any means, but I am getting better at keeping my focus on God and God's goodness when the bad times hit. May His Spirit encourage your heart as you faithfully strive to keep your focus on Him rather than on yourself.

Dear heavenly Father, how I thank You for caring for me. Your Word tells me that You are near to those who have a broken heart. That truth comforts me. Thank You for never leaving me and never relaxing your hold on me. Amen.

Day 5: Held Close in Suffering

Focus: Encouragement for Those Who Are Hurting

Scripture:

And He said to her, "Daughter, your faith has made you well. Go in peace, and be healed of your affliction."

Mark 5:34

We've spent days thinking about her, this desperate-for-healing woman making her way to Jesus. We've considered how she felt about her sickness. We've thought about how others viewed her during these years of being socially unacceptable and unclean. There were evidently many negative physical, emotional, and societal ramifications to her plight. We've imagined how she felt as she was healed, along with her trepidation of confessing to Jesus that *she* was the one who had touched His robe. But today we're coming to the sweetest part—the words of Jesus pronouncing His blessing upon her.

Remember how she fell before Jesus with fear and trembling? What do you think was going through her mind during those moments?

Do you think she was surprised by Jesus' response (Mark 5:34)?

Oh, the relief that must have flooded her soul with the sound of His words! Jesus did not publicly scold her or dismiss her with disapproval. No, indeed. Instead He responded with great compassion. He noticed her shakiness, and yet with a strong and gentle response He blessed her. My friend, let this visual play across your mind and sink into your heart. When you come to Jesus, He's always full of compassion to embrace you. His love is unconditional and steady. We can affirm with the psalmist,

Whenever I am afraid,
I will trust in You.
Psalm 56:3

Human fears are natural responses to the jolts of life. From little snags of panic to giant episodes of sheer fright, these fears can shatter your peace in an instant.

Circle the areas in which you've experienced fear:

family/children concerns   **health issues**   **job situation**

finances   **future outcomes**   **making a presentation**

confessing a wrongdoing   **decision making**   **struggles with spouse**

other: _____

Below, write Psalm 56:3 from two different translations.

Which translation speaks most personally to you? Why?

The psalmist encourages us to replace our earthly fears with trust in God. I tucked Psalm 56:3 into my memory files a long time ago. On many occasions, this verse has redirected my focus away from the defeater of my soul to the Source of my strength.

There's another fear, however, that I've often seen in God's children that causes me concern. This fear is misplaced and often keeps those who are experiencing it from emptying their hearts to the Lord and saying what's really on their minds. They are afraid of offending or displeasing God in some way. Or, if they are angry at God, they fear it would be unholy to tell Him so.

Psalm 56:3 covers this kind of fear as well. You can trust God with the secret anguish of your heart. You can even trust Him with your displeasure of what He's allowing in your life. Not placing these issues before God is sweeping them under the proverbial rug of "I'll think about this later." And that *later* gets placed on your shelf of things to address someday. Meanwhile, you don't experience the peace that is yours as God's child.

Here's a question that has an obvious answer, but I'll ask it anyway. Doesn't He know what's going on in your mind and heart whether you tell Him or not?

My friend, as I hope we will glean from this Scripture, there's nothing we can't or shouldn't take to the Lord. This woman who feared being reproached by Jesus models for us how to push through such fears by talking to Him and then receiving His blessing.

Have you ever been afraid to express your true feelings to God? If so, take a moment right now to talk to Him about it. Lay your feelings before Him, no matter what they are. Trust Him by faith to receive this offering from your heart. Now, expect to hear from Him in your soul. Make some notes below.

If you'll let Him, Christ will turn your trembling into triumphing. He longs to encourage you in your faith and communication with Him. He longs to reassure you just as He reassured our sister from long ago. His blessing to her:

> And He said to her, "Daughter, your **faith** has made you **well**. Go in **peace**, and be healed of your affliction."
>
> Mark 5:34 (emphasis added)

Let's dig deeper into this Scripture by taking a look at three key words. We'll decipher their Greek meanings in the context of this verse to get a firmer grasp on what these words of Jesus have to say to us right here and right now.

faith (*pistis*): reliance upon Christ[4]
well (*sōzō*): saved, made whole[5]
peace (*eirēnē*): peace, quietness, rest[6]

I encourage you to receive and move forward in this same blessing, applying it to your present suffering. Hear your Savior who loves you with great tenderness and compassion saying to you,

"Daughter, your reliance upon Me is saving you and making you whole. Now be at rest, quiet, and peaceful."

If you are fortunate to not be going through difficult times right now, then tuck these words away in your heart so that you can draw strength from them when the trials hit.

I just don't understand…

As a mother, it hurts to have my son suddenly diagnosed with MS at the prime of his life. He is a strong Christian, and it just doesn't feel fair that God would allow this to happen. I know God is purposeful in all He does, but it still hurts watching my strong son suffer physically. It hurts considering that my dreams for him may not be God's dreams. I've been reminded to focus on worshiping God instead of being consumed with fear. I know that God is loving and that I can find rest in Him. He is worthy of my worship no matter what life brings.

~Anonymous

The heartache and confusion in this mother's heart are real and understandable. In her letter to me, she lays out the dreams she has always had for her son. In addition to grieving for him, she grieves for his wife and children as they walk through this trial. She sees the life of her happy, athletic, and active son taking a side-road to a life that does not promise as much earthly joy as she had counted on for her child. She, a strong Christian, expressed anger that God would allow this in her son's life.

Have you ever been derailed by the sudden onset of some type of suffering— whether in the life of a friend or family member or in your own life? If so, what were some issues that consumed you?

Life is full of a variety of catastrophes: sickness, relational problems, job insecurities or dissatisfaction, health issues, caregiving dilemmas, and death.

Personally, I believe it's okay to ask God why. Notice I said *ask* Him, not *demand* that He give you an answer. I believe this because, as our loving heavenly Father, God wants us to bring every question, concern, outrage—*everything*—to Him. When I do this, I address Him in reverence and holy fear, not the ranting and raving of an immature child.

I'll also be quick to add my name to the list of those who have perpetually asked why, and still have no biblical answer. To this I've heard some say, "God doesn't owe you any explanation." Although true, that's not comforting to me when I hear it. I cannot imagine God responding to my heartache in that way.

I've come to accept the fact that there's a mystery to suffering that I'll never quite understand, and I'm okay with that. In my spirit I've been given a "cease and desist" order to stop going after the *why* and start focusing on the *Who*! I trust God, and I love Him. At this stage of my life, I'm pulling back from over analyzing and interpreting my or another's suffering. That's liberating for me. Reaching the conclusion that I don't have to know the *why* of suffering gives me more time and energy to reach out to others with the compassion of Jesus.

What are your thoughts about not having to know the *why* of suffering? Do you see this as a biblical attitude or not? Explain.

The Bible teaches us to reach out to those who need encouragement. It can be a tricky area, though. Sometimes while our hearts are right on track, the message gets convoluted when we try to communicate with others. Take a look at the following examples of what I call weird attempts to cheer somebody up.

> You could have broken both legs.
> At least you had the holidays with him.
> Look on the positive side.
> Don't you think there's a message in here somewhere?
> She's in a better place.
> You'll understand it when you get to heaven.
> Nobody said life was fair.
> Believe me—I know how you feel.

> And my all-time favorite: It could always be worse.

This topic of suffering is a heavy one. My intention is to bring a smile to your face with the above list. It's true I've heard them all, but I'm well aware that these sentiments are usually offered from genuine folks longing to bring encouragement. Maybe you've voiced a couple of them yourself. We've all been in the place of feeling awkward when trying to help another going through a trial. It's just hard to know what to say at times, right? That's why I feel it's important to spend a little time here.

Paul writes, "Therefore encourage one another and build each other up" (1 Thessalonians 5:11a NIV). Since we are called to be encouragers, it's important to explore this area.

Here are my thoughts on suffering etiquette. The above list includes things *not* to say, while those that follow are very appropriate to voice to a hurting person.

I'm here for you.

Is there a way I can help you get through this?

You're not alone.

Help me understand how you feel.

It's okay to feel this way.

I'm so sorry you're hurting.

I'm especially praying for you right now.

May I pray with you right now? (And then do it!)

Write several others:

As we conclude our week's study on suffering, I'd like to focus on the first part of Jesus' blessing: "Daughter, your faith has made you well" (Mark 5:34a).

This declaration from our Lord excites and encourages my heart! He was addressing a woman who was reaching out to Him for the first time. She was a novice at interacting with Jesus. We don't even know for a fact if her faith was in His clothing or in Him; and yet Jesus lovingly commended her for her *faith*.

What does this have to do with us today?

In a print or online Bible dictionary, look up the word *faith* and write the meaning below:

The message is clear to me. I don't need to have the right words or even understand the circumstances. I just reach for Him, rely on Him, and trust in His perfect will. This statement frees me from getting tongue-tied in my prayers or weary when I don't know how best to approach Him.

Oh, the simplicity of the love of Jesus! It's this very simplicity that says, "It's not about the amount of your faith but where you place your faith!"

The subject of suffering is surely inexhaustible. We could spend many more weeks exploring pain and suffering here on planet earth. But thanks be to God: one day it will all be over. For the child of God, there will be no more tears and no more hurts. That's not merely a nice sentiment; it's a promise!

And God shall wipe away all tears from their eyes; and there shall be no more death, neither sorrow, nor crying, neither shall there be any more pain: for the former things are passed away.

Revelation 21:4 KJV

Today's Touchpoint

It's always appropriate to share Scripture with those in pain. In fact, the longer I live and the more suffering I experience and see, I'd say Scripture is the best way we can encourage one another!

I've listed some encouraging Scripture references below. Look them up and spend some time reflecting on these promises of God. Indicate below or in a journal those that are particularly meaningful to you—along with others. A Bible concordance will help you to identify many more Scriptures of comfort and encouragement found in God's Word.

Numbers 6:26   **Isaiah 41:10**
Deuteronomy 31:6   **John 14:27**
Psalm 27:1   **Romans 15:13**
Psalm 29:11   **Philippians 4:6-7**
Psalm 46:1   **2 Thessalonians 2:16-17**

Dear heavenly Father, I thank You right now for this dear woman whose life You've highlighted for us in Your Word. I thank You for her example in showing us that desperation is a positive place when it leads us to You. Please, Lord, remind me that I never have reason to fear or be dismayed because You are my God. You will always help me and keep me steady within the grasp of Your righteous right hand. I love You. Amen.

Week 3
Video Viewer Guide

• • • • • • • • • • • • • • • • • • •

Now a certain woman had a flow of blood for twelve years, and had suffered many things from many physicians. She had spent all that she had and was no better, but rather grew worse. When she heard about Jesus, she came behind Him in the crowd and touched His garment. For she said, "If only I may touch His clothes, I shall be made well."

Mark 5:25-28 NKJV

You meet Jesus _____ the _____.

"You're _____ when you're at the _____ of your rope.

With less of you there is more of God and his rule."

Matthew 5:3 *The Message*

_____ is a great place when it leads you to the heart of God.

"These things I have spoken to you, that in Me you may have peace. In the world you will have tribulation; but be of good cheer, I have overcome the world."

John 16:33 NKJV

When you are in that place of desperation, _____ God to _____ to you.

For He Himself has said, "I will never leave you nor forsake you."
Hebrews 13:5b NKJV

Don't stop _____ to Him.

"Fear not, for I am with you;
Be not dismayed, for I am your God.
I will strengthen you,
Yes, I will help you,
I will uphold you with My righteous right hand."
Isaiah 41:10 NKJV

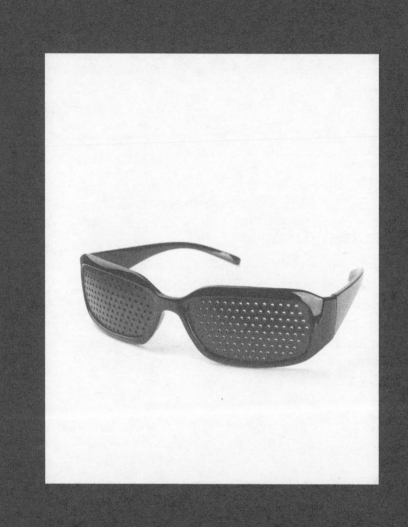

Week 4
The Woman at the Well
When You Feel Ordinary

Her Story

³ He left Judea and departed again to Galilee. ⁴ But He needed to go through Samaria.

⁵ So He came to a city of Samaria which is called Sychar, near the plot of ground that Jacob gave to his son Joseph. ⁶ Now Jacob's well was there. Jesus therefore, being wearied from His journey, sat thus by the well. It was about the sixth hour.

⁷ A woman of Samaria came to draw water. Jesus said to her, "Give Me a drink." ⁸ For His disciples had gone away into the city to buy food.

⁹ Then the woman of Samaria said to Him, "How is it that You, being a Jew, ask a drink from me, a Samaritan woman?" For Jews have no dealings with Samaritans.

¹⁰ Jesus answered and said to her, "If you knew the gift of God, and who it is who says to you, 'Give Me a drink,' you would have asked Him, and He would have given you living water."

¹¹ The woman said to Him, "Sir, You have nothing to draw with, and the well is deep. Where then do You get that living water? ¹² Are You greater than our father Jacob, who gave us the well, and drank from it himself, as well as his sons and his livestock?"

¹³ Jesus answered and said to her, "Whoever drinks of this water will thirst again, ¹⁴ but whoever drinks of the water that I shall give him will never thirst. But the water that I shall give him will become in him a fountain of water springing up into everlasting life."

¹⁵ The woman said to Him, "Sir, give me this water, that I may not thirst, nor come here to draw."

¹⁶ Jesus said to her, "Go, call your husband, and come here."

¹⁷ The woman answered and said, "I have no husband."

Jesus said to her, "You have well said, 'I have no husband,' ¹⁸ for you have had five husbands, and the one whom you now have is not your husband; in that you spoke truly."

¹⁹ The woman said to Him, "Sir, I perceive that You are a prophet. ²⁰ Our fathers worshiped on this mountain, and you Jews say that in Jerusalem is the place where one ought to worship."

²¹ Jesus said to her, "Woman, believe Me, the hour is coming when you will neither on this mountain, nor in Jerusalem, worship the Father. ²² You worship what you do not know; we know what we worship, for salvation is of the Jews. ²³ But the hour is coming, and now is, when the true worshipers will worship the Father in spirit and truth; for the Father is seeking such to worship Him. ²⁴ God is Spirit, and those who worship Him must worship in spirit and truth."

²⁵ The woman said to Him, "I know that Messiah is coming" (who is called Christ). "When He comes, He will tell us all things."

²⁶ Jesus said to her, "I who speak to you am He."

John 4:3-26

Her Name: *Ordinary*

Our anonymous sister from Samaria came from a race despised by the Jews. Her conversation with Jesus appears in the Scriptures shortly after His encounter with Nicodemus (John 3:1-21), who was a Pharisee and prominent member of the Sanhedrin. I am simply captivated by the layout of God's Word! I see a holy design of God's grace in the arrangement of these "side by side" stories. The first dialogue was with one who was highly respected; the second was with an outcast. But to Jesus they appeared the same.

My friend, are you living with the notion that there is nothing special about you? If so, you're surely looking at it from the world's perspective, not the Lord's. I'm so pumped about this week's content. As I stand before my computer right now, I'm pausing to pray for you. If you will drink deeply from this living water, He'll change your ordinary into His extraordinary!

Memory Verse

I will praise You, for I am fearfully and wonderfully made;
Marvelous are Your works,
And that my soul knows very well.

Psalm 139:14

Meditating on this verse will help you celebrate who you are in the heart of God. I encourage you to consider it often, thanking your heavenly Father for His wonderful handiwork in *you*!

Day 1: A Divine Appointment

Focus: Significant to God

Scripture:

³He left Judea and departed again to Galilee. ⁴But He needed to go through Samaria.
⁵So He came to a city of Samaria which is called Sychar, near the plot of ground that Jacob gave to his son Joseph.

John 4:3-5

Jesus and his followers left Judea and headed north to Galilee. I'm sure the disciples were intent on getting to their destination when they set out. Still young in their relationship with Jesus, they had not yet grown accustomed to the way He interrupted schedules and plans to reach out to the hurting. (Last week's study is a prime example of this very thing, as He took time to heal the hemorrhaging woman on the way to Jairus' house.) Yes, they had much to learn about His heart of love for all whom His Father had created. And so it was that Jesus continued teaching them on this subject in an unlikely classroom found in Samaria. His interaction at Jacob's well with a woman who surely must have felt ordinary and overlooked can help us understand His thoughts about us when we feel the same.

Here's a present-day sharing from a girlfriend about an encounter that left her feeling like a nobody.

I was never exceptional in my abilities or my appearance. I mostly went quietly about my daily life, never realizing my condition until one Saturday afternoon many years ago. I was working concessions at the local movie theater when in walked a flamboyant young man who graduated high school a couple of years ahead of me. After we had chatted a bit, conversation turned to high school friends, and I mentioned my best friend's name. He responded "Really? I had a huge crush on her, but I don't recall ever seeing you!" I explained to him that it is hard to see the moon when the sun is out! That's when I knew. . . .I was anonymous.

~Anonymous

Listen, my sister: If you're in relationship with Jesus Christ, then one day every experience of feeling ordinary and being dismissed by others will simply lose its hold over you. In fact, my guess is that we won't even remember those times! My sense is that when such encounters occur, God thinks, "I can't wait until she sees who she really is!"

Have you ever felt *anonymous* because of your appearance or social status? If so, circle the words and phrases below that describe your feelings at the time.

unimportant	overlooked	misfit
no benefit to anyone	nothing to contribute	not good enough
unknown	uncared for	lost in a crowd
unattractive	unnoticed	low self-esteem
unlikable	ordinary	"less than"

other: _____

My friend, tears come to my eyes as I write these descriptions. Nobody likes to feel overlooked, discarded, or worthless. It hurts, doesn't it? The reality is you don't have to feel this way—because you're not! I'm thrilled to travel through this passage in John 4 with you this week. Together we are going to dig into God's truth about who we are in Jesus. And what He thinks about you is the only opinion that matters!

Back to the classroom . . .

Without understanding the religious climate of the day, it would certainly seem that Samaria would be a likely place for Jesus and His disciples to stop, rest, and talk with the locals. This region was located about halfway between Judea and Galilee, and going through the area certainly was a direct route, geographically speaking. It was not a spot, however, where Jews typically travelled or enjoyed hanging out. In fact, most avoided it, adding extra miles to their journey in order to travel around it.

The Samaritans were a mixed race of people that began after Israel divided hundreds of years before Jesus' time. After Assyria conquered Israel, the remaining Jews and Assyrians intermarried. These Jews then began worshiping the Assyrians' pagan idols alongside the One God of Israel. Walls of bitterness and hatred arose between the full-blooded monotheistic Jews and the Samaritans because of their intermarriage and worship practices. Prejudices grew and attitudes steeled. As a whole, Samaritans and Jews detested one another.

But Jesus "**needed** to go through Samaria" (John 4:4, emphasis added)! The Greek word translated as "needed" is *dei*, which means "it is necessary."[1] It's the same context as the words Jesus used when he said, "Did you not know that I must be about My Father's business?" (Luke 2:49b).

Jesus knew there was something significant that was about to happen at this very spot between Judea and Galilee—in Samaria! Right in the middle of an ordinary day, as Jesus and His disciples traveled through a land where hatred between two races was the accepted norm, a divine encounter was about to take place.

In your own words, define or describe a *divine* encounter:

Have you had a personal experience of a divine encounter in your life? If so, describe it below:

Recap the facts we've covered thus far by completing the following sentences:

Jesus left _____ and headed north to _____.

He and His disciples stopped in _____, which was about halfway.

Jesus _____ to go through Samaria.

Factually speaking, Jesus was moving through His earthly timeline and was right on schedule as he travelled through Samaria to do His Father's will. The meeting between "the woman at the well" and Jesus was no accidental encounter. It was a planned divine encounter.

Review Psalm 139:16, a verse we read earlier in our study. What does the psalmist say about the days of your life in this verse?

Jesus knew this day would come in the life of the Samaritan woman who came to draw water from the well. He knew her hurts, the longings of her heart, and where she was trying to find satisfaction. He knew she needed fulfillment and purpose for living. He waited for the conversation that would begin to heal her heart and give her a fresh outlook on life. The psalmist's words were true for her, and they're true for us.

I will praise You
because I have been remarkably and wonderfully made.
Your works are wonderful,
and I know this very well.

Psalm 139:14 HCSB

How often we totally dismiss the message in this verse!

According to this psalm, how have you been made?

God's works (in you) are described as _____.

What should be your response to Him?

On the scale below, rate your typical view of yourself.

1	3	5
detest who I am	**okay with myself**	**in awe of God's work**

I'm not suggesting you pack up for an ego trip, but I am encouraging you to take some time to marvel at God's work in your body and soul. Unless you regularly do this, you will wander down the road of self-abasement when things don't go well for you. The more you get into that pattern, the deeper you dig trenches of self-pity and the like. Look at the definition below. Have you ever fallen into this trap?

> *self-abasement* – humiliation of oneself, especially as a result of guilt, shame, or the like

Consider this scenario. In a recent "parade of tables" event hosted by your church's women's ministry, the table you decorated did not make the top ten list singled out in the church bulletin. You worked really hard, and secretly you were hoping to be noticed. Your table not getting attention translates into this kind of self-talk: *I am not good enough, creative enough, or working hard enough to make the grade.*

Stick with me here. When I taught middle-school girls for many years, I was continually patching wounded egos. And being a grown-up middle-schooler myself, I know that many of these same feelings hang around throughout our adult years. Our natural thought process is to go in the direction I've just described. We must be deliberate about keeping God's view of us in the forefront of our thinking and processing.

Using the previous example, God's truth is simply this: *I am significant, remarkable, and wonderfully made whether my table is chosen or not. It would be nice if it was, but if not, it does not affect how I view myself through God's eyes.*

If you are not one who is harassed with this kind of negative thinking about self from time to time, please forgive my elementary elaboration. Perhaps by understanding the inner climate of others you know, you'll become better skilled at reaching out to them in more Christ-like ways. The bottom line is this: in order to rise above feelings of insignificance in the eyes of others, it's critical to understand our significance to God!

I have long been fascinated with the prayer of Jesus found in John 17. It gives such an intimate look at His love for His Father and His Father's children.

Enjoy reading John 17 right now. Ask the Holy Spirit to open your heart to the heart of Jesus as you read.

What are several thoughts of Jesus that catch your attention in this passage?

What does Jesus ask the Father to do in verse 17?

Sanctify – to make holy, to set apart for sacred use

How does it make you feel to know that Jesus is praying for you, asking the Father to show you, by His Word, how to live a holy life that is set apart for Him?

My favorite verse in John 17 is verse 24. I especially like the Amplified Bible translation:

> *Father, I desire that they also whom You have entrusted to Me [as Your gift to Me] may be with Me where I am, so that they may see My glory, which You have given Me [Your love gift to Me]; for You loved Me before the foundation of the world.*

It set my heart on edge the first time this verse took hold of me. *I am a love gift from God the Father to Jesus, His Son!* And so are you!

In John 17:26, what does Jesus specifically pray for us?

If we can train ourselves to focus on the fact that we are a "gift" to Jesus Christ from God the Father, then our entire emotional infrastructure will be built on the truth of God's Word rather than on faulty perceptions. I've found the best way to keep that truth welling up in my heart is to remember that Jesus is praying for me to get it!

Today's Touchpoint

Scripture doesn't say exactly how this anonymous woman— I've chosen the name *Ordinary* for her—viewed herself, but we can read between the lines. Based on your experiences and emotions as a woman and the background of this passage, what self-perceptions do you think she was likely to have?

Now, my friend, what about you? As we close today's time together, my prayer is that you will be open to the tender touch of Jesus in the areas He reveals. Go back and look over those phrases you circled in the beginning of today's lesson. In light of each one, pray this week's memory verse. Remember that just as Jesus "*needed* to go through Samaria," He *needs* to come to you. In other words, it's necessary to Him that He interact with you, encourage you, and give you His living water to bring fresh vision to your life. He's orchestrating a divine appointment just for you.

I'm joining you in spending moments with our Lord, talking over some back-issues of my life that have flung a shadow over my psyche. I'm asking our Holy Spirit to touch your heart and mine, revealing the Father's love in fresh new ways. It's a choice we have, dear friend, to see ourselves in the way our Lord sees us. We can do it, though, with acceptance and faith!

Dear heavenly Father, it staggers me to think that I could possibly be a lovegift from You to Your Son. Thank You for seeking me out to love. I feel so unworthy and so unlovely much of the time. Will You help me to grasp the truth that Your love for me is based on the perfection of Jesus, not on my own worthiness? I open my heart to You. Help me to discover that I'm never overlooked by You and that each moment of my life is significant to You. Thank You for making me in such a wonderful way. I marvel in Your work, and I love You. Amen.

Day 2: Jesus Encounter

Focus: The Nature of Our Lord

Scripture:

⁶*Now Jacob's well was there. Jesus therefore, being wearied from His journey, sat thus by the well. It was about the sixth hour.*

⁷ *A woman of Samaria came to draw water. Jesus said to her, "Give Me a drink."* ⁸ *For His disciples had gone away into the city to buy food.*

John 4:6-8

I accepted the fact many years ago that Jesus came to earth as fully God, fully man.

> *The Word became flesh*
> *and made his home among us.*
> *We have seen his glory,*
> *glory like that of a father's only son,*
> *full of grace and truth.*
> John 1:14 CEB

The language "the Word became flesh" is so simple, but its reality is so mindboggling! Just think about it: the sovereign God was contained inside a physical body. Take a few moments to ponder the following passages.

For each Scripture, record the phrase that supports the given statement.

Luke 2:7 – He was born:

Luke 2:40 – He grew:

John 4:6 – He got tired:

John 19:28 – He got thirsty:

Matthew 4:2 – He got hungry:

Luke 24:39 – He had a real body after His resurrection:

In addition to His physical body, Jesus clearly had emotions.

List an emotion found in each Scripture:

Matthew 8:10 _____

Matthew 26:38 _____

John 11:33-35 _____

John 12:27 _____

Christ experienced every aspect of being human, including both the physical and emotional.

Pause with me for a moment to thank Him for this glorious and astounding truth. Ask the Holy Spirit to give you fresh adoration and awe as you contemplate this holy reality, and record your thoughts below.

When I grasp the truth of Christ's humanity, I understand why He was weary. But as I read John 4:6-8, a question arose as I thought about His tiredness. We're told that while He was resting, His disciples went into the city to buy food. As I initially mulled it over, I wondered why there was no mention of the disciples being weary. It was around noon, and they'd all been traveling together for some time. As I continued my research, here's what I discovered.

The Greek word *kopiao* is used in this passage. It means "to grow weary, tired, exhausted (with toil or burdens or grief)."[2] In addition to being tired physically, this word also means to become emotionally and mentally fatigued—as occurs when we are weighed down with burdens or grief. It occurred to me that perhaps Jesus was not only physically tired but also emotionally and mentally tired.

Thinking back to times when I've experienced mental or emotional fatigue, I recall that the tiredness and weariness was even greater, it seemed, than just mere physical exhaustion.

Describe in a few words or phrases what it feels like to be emotionally and mentally fatigued.

What are some possible reasons that Jesus could have felt emotionally and mentally exhausted at this time in His earthly life?

Though we do not know all that may have contributed to Jesus' tiredness in this moment, here's what we do know: He was weary from traveling, so He sat by the well. As He rested, a Samaritan woman came to draw water in the heat of the day. I picture her carrying her water jug. Usual times for gathering water were morning and evening, and yet she approached at a time when others were not typically there. Speculation is that she was shunned and rejected by the other women in her area because of her immorality.

What does Luke 15:2 say about Jesus and His interaction with sinners?

According to Romans 3:23, who has sinned—who are "sinners"?

Is there any indication in this verse that some are more sinful than others?

Though Scripture tells us that *all* have sinned, in our biased thinking and particular circumstances we often *rank* the sins of humanity. That is not biblical, nor is it God's thinking.

I want to ask you something, dear friend. Have you ever gone out of your way to avoid a person or group because you felt rejected by them? If so, you're not alone! Sometimes it's just easier to keep to yourself instead of being around people who cause you to dredge up negative emotions, right? Perhaps that's why this woman came during the part of the day when she knew others would not be there.

Here's the truth of the matter. When you said "yes" to Jesus, you were *justified*. That means you were declared innocent and righteous before God. Through studying the Bible and praying and having an ongoing relationship with Christ, you are being *sanctified*—becoming holy. And one day you will be *glorified* with a new body and new heart, just like Christ's. The problem with earthly living is that we are not in that glorified state yet. So, all Christians struggle with sin. But I'll add quickly: if we love the Lord, the goal is to get better and better at *not* sinning! The apostle Paul gives this advice on pursuing righteousness:

> *Instead, pursue righteous living, faithfulness, love, and peace. Enjoy the companionship of those who call on the Lord with pure hearts.*
> 2 Timothy 2:22b NLT

As I think about this woman and her "sin issue," I'm not downplaying her sin but reminding us that her sin is between her and the Lord—just as our sins are between us and the Lord. It's a great practice to focus on the Lord's forgiveness and love, rather than letting the negative judgments of others weigh us down. Maintaining this focus will also keep us from critiquing the sins of others.

As she approached, Jesus began a conversation with her. In doing so, He broke three customs of Jewish culture:

1. *He spoke to a woman.* During Jesus' day, the status and freedoms of women were severely limited by the law. They had little or no authority in the roles they played. According to custom, they also were considered inferior to men. This John 4 passage is one of many showing that Jesus viewed men and women as equals standing side by side before God.

2. *She was Samaritan.* We've already explored how the Samaritans were a group traditionally despised by the Jews. In his commentary Matthew Henry states, "It was the pride of the Jews that they would endure any hardship rather than be beholden to a Samaritan."[3]

3. *He asked her for a drink of water.* Because of the division between Jews and Samaritans, the law stated that using a cup or eating utensil from this woman would render Jesus ceremonially unclean.

Jesus' request for a drink of water gives me such pause for considering His humility. He, being God in the flesh, became physically thirsty and asked for water. From His physical need, He began a discourse with this dear woman about the *water of life*. He was always willing to set His glory down right in the middle of humanity to help others understand about God's love.

When I consider Jesus' request and its relevance for us today, I think about what God desires from us. Though God does not have "needs" that He asks us to meet, He does desire a relationship with us; and we can bring Him pleasure in this relationship. In other words, we can give Him a drink by offering Him our love and worship.

> *The LORD is pleased only*
> *with those who worship him*
> *and trust his love.*
> Psalm 147:11 CEV

We can worship the Lord through our words and our actions.

And whatever you do in word or deed, do *all in the name of the Lord Jesus, giving thanks to God the Father through him. (Colossians 3:17)*

What does Colossians 3:17 say about everything we speak or do?

Could you also consider the following as ways to give Christ a drink? What others can you add to this list?

Talking to Him throughout your day

Taking extra time for sharing kindness

Going out of your way to speak to someone who seems to be unnoticed

Spending time with those who have no one to talk to

Others:

It humbles and delights me to think that I might bring Jesus pleasure. Years ago I began telling Him how much I appreciate the things He does for me. I truly sense His pleasure in receiving these genuine thoughts springing forth from my heart. The more I thank Him, the more overcome with gratitude I seem to be.

As for the woman at the well, I believe she was a bit taken aback when Jesus spoke to her. His disciples were too, it seems. I find a bit of humor in the unfolding of this scenario. We read that when they returned, they were amazed that He was talking with a woman (see John 4:27). I can almost see their faces and body language as they expressed their surprise.

Jesus was full of surprises, wasn't He? While they were in the city buying food to replenish the physical body, He was offering a woman true sustenance—the living water that nurtures the soul and spirit. To Jesus, the spiritual always trumped the physical. What an example for us to live by!

Today's Touchpoint

In today's lesson we mentioned three words important to Christian doctrine: *justification, sanctification,* and *glorification.* These concepts form a foundation for our Christian beliefs and faith. Understanding and applying them to our daily walk in Christ will keep us thinking and behaving victoriously.

Using a print or online Bible dictionary, define each of these words as it refers to your relationship with Jesus Christ.

Justification

Sanctification

Glorification

Read the following Scriptures and draw a line to match each one to the doctrine that it highlights:

Romans 3:23-24   Sanctification

John 17:17   Glorification

Romans 8:18   Justification

How does understanding these truths of your reality in Christ give you encouragement for a current issue you are facing?

Dear heavenly Father, words don't come easily as I try to thank You for coming to earth and putting on a physical body of flesh and blood. It touches me that You would be willing to empty Yourself and take on body and soul like those You created. Thank You for loving me this much. Doctrine can get confusing to me at times, but help me to understand the basics of being justified, sanctified, and glorified. Knowing these truths helps me find joy in You instead of depending on others to provide that joy. I know You don't need anything from me, but thank You for finding pleasure in my company. Thank You for allowing me to serve You. I love You, Lord. Amen.

Day 3: The Water of Life

Focus: A New Thirst

Scripture:

⁹Then the woman of Samaria said to Him, "How is it that You, being a Jew, ask a drink from me, a Samaritan woman?" For Jews have no dealings with Samaritans.

¹⁰ Jesus answered and said to her, "If you knew the gift of God, and who it is who says to you, 'Give Me a drink,' you would have asked Him, and He would have given you living water."

¹¹ The woman said to Him, "Sir, You have nothing to draw with, and the well is deep. Where then do You get that living water? ¹² Are You greater than our father Jacob, who gave us the well, and drank from it himself, as well as his sons and his livestock?"

¹³ Jesus answered and said to her, "Whoever drinks of this water will thirst again, ¹⁴ but whoever drinks of the water that I shall give him will never thirst. But the water that I shall give him will become in him a fountain of water springing up into everlasting life."

John 4:9-14

Our anonymous sister surely eyed Jesus with curiosity during their dialogue. They had a verbal exchange about how He, a Jewish man, would even speak to her, much less ask her for a drink of water. There was something about this man that drew her deeper into conversation. Then Jesus pressed further in with these words: "If you knew the gift of God, and who it is who says to you, 'Give Me a drink,' you would have asked Him, and He would have given you living water" (v. 10). Now she was puzzled—perhaps slightly amused—replying, "Sir, You have nothing to draw with, and the well is deep. Where then do You get that living water?" (v. 11). This is a great place in this passage to stop and reflect.

Fill in the blanks below to review the facts in our story so far. Don't skip this step!

On the way to Galilee, Jesus and company stop in _____.

While the disciples go to the city for food, Jesus rests beside a _____.

A woman approaches to draw _____.

Jesus breaks three Jewish customs: He talks to a _____ who is a _____, and he asks her for a _____ of _____.

The woman is surprised because Jews have no dealings with _____.

They continue in dialogue, and the woman comments that Jesus has nothing with which to draw water and the well is deep. She asks, "Sir where then do You get that _____ _____?"

I want you not only to catch the simplicity of this story but also to apply it; that's the reason for the review. I've seen this scenario played out on many occasions. Step into the present day. A Christian begins a dialogue with Jesus. It may sound something like this:

> Lord, I know I've messed up my life. I've made many mistakes that I cannot undo. I know You have a plan for me, but I'm not seeing a way out of my mess. Your Word says, "Ask and you will receive." Well, I've asked over and over, Lord, and I have yet to hear Your answers. How is it that You would have anything special for the likes of me anyway? I know the Bible says that I have a hope and a future, but . . .

> "Sir, You have nothing to draw with, and the well is deep. Where then do You get that living water?"

My friend, let's bring the application home by taking a closer look at our own confidence in the abilities of Jesus. Can you think of a personal situation where you talked with the Lord and told Him you trusted Him, but secretly you thought, *He's not in touch practically with my reality of the moment*? In other words, "Lord, You have nothing to draw with." This storyline might involve family issues, health and finance matters, or personal problems. Whatever the situation, there seems to be no sign of help. "The well is deep. Where then do You get that living water?" So many times in my life I have longed for the practicality of Jesus to rush in and save the day!

If only He would tell me what to do, I'd gladly do it, I've thought. Ever felt that way?

I remember such an experience during my final year of teaching. For some time I had felt the Holy Spirit's tug to step out in faith to the next phase of God's plan for me, which involved writing and beginning a ministry to women. I knew it would be a big change, and I knew I was walking away from the security I enjoyed in my sixth grade classroom. Spring arrived that year, along with the contract for the next teaching year, awaiting my signature. With the decision looming before me, I begged God to show me the handwriting on His holy wall. My version of "Sir, You have nothing to draw with, and the well is deep. Where then do You get that living water" played out like this: "Lord, You are not here physically, dealing with this decision. This is deep stuff because what I choose is going to affect the rest of my life. Where do I find Your answer?"

Have you ever pleaded with God to give you His answer? If so, how did you feel in that moment?

Below are some possible scenarios. Complete those sentences that ring true for you:

I need to know _____.

*Where am I going to find*_____?

I feel so _____*and*_____.

Lord, if You don't _____,

*then*_____.

Other: _____

Knowing what we know about the woman at the well, which of the following do you think she might have thought?

_____ *I see nothing in His hands; how could He draw water?*
_____ *What is living water, anyway?*
_____ *Does He think He's greater than Jacob?*
_____ *Was He expecting me to come here?*

_____ ***Does He know my lifestyle?***
_____ ***Why is He talking to me?***

I bet there were some real questions forming in her mind by this point in the conversation. Our questions are of a different sort. We know about Jesus and His living water. But we don't always understand how to take hold of it. So how do we emerge victoriously from those tangled times of life when we desperately need Jesus to practically show up and tell us what to do?

His answer to our Samaritan girlfriend is the same one that He gives to us:

> *"Whoever drinks of this water will thirst again."*
> John 4:13b

Panicking over life's situations and becoming obsessed with knowing and making the right decisions will leave you breathless and thirsty for worldly answers. You'll begin making demands of God and feeling entitled to an answer from Him. This brings us to the second part of Jesus' answer:

> *"But whoever drinks of the water that I shall give Him will never thirst."*
> John 4:14a

Calming yourself in God's Word and in His presence will begin to quench that insatiable thirst for Him to tell you the answer and will help you find sanity in Him instead. He is the Living Water—not only for the moment but for all of eternity:

> *But the water that I shall give him will become in Him a fountain of water springing up into everlasting life.*
>
> John 4:14b

Many times I've almost physically felt that fountain of water springing up inside of me as I've steadied myself and focused on Christ *being* the answer instead of Him *giving* me the answer.

You may be thinking, *What about my very real need for the very real circumstance I'm facing?* My friend, I can't speak to your "particulars." I can only testify to the faithfulness of God in walking me through the problematic times in my own life. Let me share with you the process that I've found helpful.

When I am faced with a critical decision-making opportunity—whether it is a hands-on practical matter or more of an abstract nature—I have a choice. I can steel myself in mental angst, hoping to choose rightly, or I can steep myself in God's Word and presence—the living water.

The natural response is to reason, calculate, and gather all the facts. This is being responsible, and I believe it's honoring to our Lord. After I've gathered the facts, I find it is critical to step away and allow seeking Him to replace seeking an answer. At that point it comes down to trusting in the abilities of Jesus (not my own) to see me through.

Then I approach Him in this way: "Lord, Your Word says to 'seek first the kingdom of God and His righteousness, and all these things shall be added to [me]' (Matthew 6:33). My desperate need right now is included in 'these things,' so I trust You to lead me in Your way."

Finally, I simply move forward in trust that the direction I'm taking is from Him. I believe that even if the decision I make is not the best one, He will still honor my trust in moving in the way I feel He has directed me. It all comes down to whether I'm trusting in my own abilities or trusting in the abilities of Jesus to see me through.

This process of decision-making can be outlined in three simple steps:

1. Steep yourself in God's Word and presence—the living water.
2. Gather the facts, and then seek God above seeking an answer.
3. Pray for God to lead you in His way, and trust that He will.

Write your thoughts about this three-step process of decision-making:

As we close our study today, I'd like to share one final thought about the living water Jesus spoke of in this encounter with the woman at the well. When He spoke of the water "springing up" (John 4:14), He used the Greek word *hallomai*, which means to "leap or spring up."[4] In speaking to our sister, Jesus was speaking metaphorically of the Holy Spirit springing up in the believer's life. We find the same word used in Acts 14 to describe the action of the man who was crippled from birth and healed by the Holy Spirit through Paul: "And he *leaped* and walked" (Acts. 14:10b, emphasis added).

Oh, how I need the leaping Holy Spirit to spring up within me and flow outward into my life. My friend, He longs to do the same for you. He wants to fill you with the energy and excitement for daily living that comes only from Him! He can replace the stagnant water within your soul with glorious ripples of joy.

Today's Touchpoint

This Samaritan woman recognized that the stranger by the well was a Jew. Maybe it was His dress, or it could have been His dialect. Yet He did not treat her as she would have expected, and this caught her attention. Instead, Jesus showed kindness to her by taking time to converse with her and by offering her the love of God.

It seems fitting to spend our closing moments of today's lesson in petitioning God. I'm not talking about asking Him to grant you favor, or to give you discernment over a particular matter, or to take care of your needs and the needs of your family. While all of these are *biblically permissible*, I have another kind of request in mind. Let's ask our heavenly Father to put a particular someone in our path—an ordinary someone who is typically overlooked by others, a someone with whom we can share kindness and the love of Jesus. The Holy Spirit may bring this person to mind instantly, or He may show you through the day's circumstances who this individual is. I can tell you this: every time I've made such a request of my Lord, He has been faithful to allow me an opportunity to shower someone with His love. He orchestrates the event, and I just follow His lead. May your heart be filled to overflowing as He presents you with your *Ordinary*.

Return here later to write about your encounter, or record your thoughts in a journal.

Dear Father, gradually I'm learning to love as You love. Keep me alert to the hurting and scorned around me. I'm sure that I come in contact with many on a weekly basis who feel overlooked and insignificant. Right now, Father, I boldly ask You to create an opportunity for me to share Your kindness and love. It may be a stranger I encounter when I'm at lunch, in the grocery store, or running errands. Or this person may be one You've already placed on my heart and are calling me to reach out to. Thank You, Lord, for loving me the way You do. Give me the desire to love others in Your name and with Your love. Amen.

Day 4: Conversing with Jesus

Focus: Growing in Understanding

Scripture:

¹⁵The woman said to Him, "Sir, give me this water, that I may not thirst, nor come here to draw."

¹⁶ Jesus said to her, "Go, call your husband, and come here."

¹⁷ The woman answered and said, "I have no husband."

Jesus said to her, "You have well said, 'I have no husband,' ¹⁸ for you have had five husbands, and the one whom you now have is not your husband; in that you spoke truly."

¹⁹ The woman said to Him, "Sir, I perceive that You are a prophet. ²⁰ Our fathers worshiped on this mountain, and you Jews say that in Jerusalem is the place where one ought to worship."

²¹ Jesus said to her, "Woman, believe Me, the hour is coming when you will neither on this mountain, nor in Jerusalem, worship the Father. ²² You worship what you do not know; we know what we worship, for salvation is of the Jews."

John 4:15-22

It's hard to say whether her response to Jesus regarding the water He spoke of was sincere or spoken in ridicule. It could have been . . .

Oh, please, I need your water so I won't have to come to this desolate place in the heat of the day to draw water anymore!

or

I long for this kind of water that will bring satisfaction to my life!

The commentaries I've researched differ in their interpretations of how the interaction between Jesus and this Samaritan woman played out. Personally, I love this element of God's Word. We get to suppose and imagine this part of the story. Pondering her reaction helps me to walk in her sandals and get inside of her head and heart. I've really enjoyed reflecting on the possibilities within their conversation. It has brought this passage alive to me, stimulating my awareness of the practicality and relevance of God's Word for my present day reality.

So, in your opinion, was she mocking this Jew who behaved strangely, or was she becoming genuinely interested in what this unusual man was offering?

What do you think?

There are many other passages in the Bible about which we can imagine what is not recorded for us to actually know. Another one that comes to my mind is our first nameless woman—*Judged*, who anointed Jesus with tears flowing from her heart of love. I like to imagine what it was like the moment she realized she loved the Lord. What happened in her heart and mind as she made that discovery? I have enjoyed talking to God about the way He orchestrated that circumstance.

Is this approach of meditating on God's Word inviting to you? Why or why not?

After their interchange regarding the water, the conversation takes a turn. With it, we see the grace of Jesus unfolding in these next verses. "Go, call your husband," He said. Ah, now He had her ear, for sure. He knows that she has been married five times and is not married to the man she is now living with, yet He doesn't call it to attention. With His words, He surely opens a wound in order to position her to receive His gift of grace.

Let's reflect a moment. Do you find that we are more open to hearing and embracing God's grace when a wound has been reopened? How about when some sin has been exposed? In my experience, I've always been especially drawn to Jesus at those particular times. Sometimes it's with a repenting heart; sometimes with a broken one.

Let us therefore come boldly to the throne of grace, that we may obtain mercy and find grace to help in time of need. (Hebrews 4:16)

Read Hebrews 4:16 above. What do you think this verse says about our vulnerability in approaching Jesus?

In deference to her sagging soul, Jesus simply gives a directive that initiates a response from her. "I have no husband," she states curtly—at least that is my opinion of her delivery. This suggests that she would like to keep moving along in the conversation without elaborating on this issue. I believe it's probable that the verbal exchange that follows is more than is recorded here. This verse leads me to that assumption:

> *Come, see a Man who told me all things that I ever did. Could this be the Christ?*
> John 4:29

This verse suggests that Jesus knew more about this woman than her marital history and talked with her about various aspects of her life. All of their conversation, apparently, is not for us to know.

There are some things that are better left to you and God. It gives me great comfort and joy to discuss private and personal things with God. Whether they're dreams of what's to come or thoughts that I know only He understands or feelings that I really don't care for others to know, it's an intimate sharing between the two of us.

What is your biggest barrier to this kind of One-on-one, intimate relationship with your heavenly Father? Explain your answer.

Once she admits she has no husband, Jesus responds: "You have well said, 'I have no husband,' for you have had five husbands, and the one whom you now have is not your husband; in that you spoke truly" (John 4:17b-18).

What she most likely intended as a denial and dismissal of the fact, Jesus used to bring her to conviction. You know, it's impossible to move in concert with the living water if there is unconfessed sin in your heart. I can vouch for that from personal experience.

Knowing the kindness of our Lord, I don't believe His tone is an accusing one here. He confirms the fact simply, as if to allow her conscience to state the rest. What a gentle example He sets before us in this discourse. I long to emulate His pattern of relating to others in my words and especially in my thinking. If I can get my thought life in line with His, then surely when I open my mouth His thinking will come out!

It seems that in her realization of His knowledge about her situation, her mind and heart begin to soften.

Look at verse 19. What is her perception of Jesus now?

She doesn't deny what He has said, but she is interested in carrying on the dialogue with Him.

What do you think might have happened next if Jesus had spoken harshly of her sin?

Do you believe His gentleness gave her the freedom to continue talking with Him? Elaborate on your thoughts.

What does this suggest to us about confronting others about the sin in their lives?

Jesus allows her to take the conversation where she will. So, she turns it to religion and worship. The passage implies that she knows she should worship God; she just isn't sure where and how to do this.

According to the woman, where do the Samaritans worship?

Where do the Jews worship?

Both the Jews and Samaritans agree that God should be worshipped, but her point of interest seems to be the place of worship. Earlier in the conversation she mentioned *Jacob*, and now she speaks of "our fathers." She likely thinks the ancestry of the Samaritans gives them more favor with God. Perhaps she believes that because of their lineage, the mountain where they worship is the proper and only place to approach God.

In verse 21, what is Jesus' response to her about worship?

It seems to me that Jesus is making light of the weight she is placing upon the place of worship and, at the same moment, casting a shadow on the emphasis she places upon the preference of her forefathers. He knows a time is coming when it will make no difference at all where God is worshiped. He will not be confined to a place or a group of people.

In verse 22, Jesus says salvation is of whom?

Surely Jesus is not speaking of the Jewish religion as practiced by the Pharisees and Sadducees. How could salvation come from that kind of pompous legalism? Remember that Jesus is very put-off by their style.

> *"Everything they do is for show. On their arms they wear extra wide prayer boxes with Scripture verses inside, and they wear robes with extra-long tassels. And they love to sit at the head table at banquets and in the seats of honor in the synagogues. They love to receive respectful greetings as they walk in the marketplaces, and to be called 'Rabbi.'"*
>
> Matthew 23:5-7 NLT

According to many biblical commentaries, Jesus was simply referring to the fact that He, the Messiah, was a Jew by birth, and that He would bring salvation into the world. The name Jesus means the same in Greek as the Hebrew name *Joshua*, which literally means *God is salvation*.

Record the words spoken by Gabriel to Mary in Matthew 1:21.

Jesus was leading the woman at the well to a gradual understanding that He, the Christ, was the way of salvation. His was the only plan of deliverance made available to humanity. Neither the Samaritans nor any others have the option of designing their own plan for how to be saved.

As they continued in conversation, she was thinking *physical*; Jesus was talking *spiritual*. It may have taken her a while to grasp the spiritual implications, but I like to believe that she eventually got it.

Tomorrow we'll move through the final elements of their meeting. It was a divine encounter for her—a divine model for us. Jesus moves prudently and graciously with her, not lecturing her about her morals or arguing with her about her religious beliefs. Instead, His approach keeps her engaged, asking questions, and ultimately seeking the truth—His Truth for her and for us.

Today's Touchpoint

Let's revisit the part of the conversation where this woman's emphasis was placed on *where* to worship. Think of previous places of worship from your background. Name them or simply assign numbers to them. For each one, did you perceive those attending to be more concerned with the place or with true worship?

Jot some thoughts below.

My goal in this exercise is not to cause you to be critical, only observational. In my personal experience, I confess to times of getting really caught up in the logistics of programming or creating an attractive environment. This is a fine line, agreed? It's important to plan, prepare, and set the stage. Those things add to meaningful worship experiences. But when they become the focus instead of the vehicle to carry us to the real focus, we become spiritually out of whack.

Now, think of places where you've had a worship experience with God during the past year. The places can be here, there, anywhere, everywhere. God is not limited to specific areas!

Share a couple of thoughts about your worship experience in each of these places. You may share your own reflections below , or answer the following questions.

Was this a spontaneous moment of worship?

What prompted your worship?

Were you alone with God, or were others involved?

Did you feel spiritually connected with God?

Did this time with your heavenly Father lead you to begin new patterns of worship?

How were you different as a result of this particular worship experience?

My friend, may we be forever changed by these truths we are taking into our hearts. Looking deeply into the lives of these nameless women is helping me grow. The reality of God's love for them is making a strong impact on my life. The way He loved them is the way He loves me and you. How glorious!

My heavenly Father, I can't wait to see You face to face and tell You how grateful I am for Your love. Thank You for reaching through the lives of these women right into the depths of my heart. I'm humbled and honored that You should love me the way You do. Thank You, and I love You. Amen.

Day 5: Choosing Extraordinary

Focus: Being Known and Loved

Scripture:

²³But the hour is coming, and now is, when the true worshipers will worship the Father in spirit and truth; for the Father is seeking such to worship Him. ²⁴God is Spirit, and those who worship Him must worship in spirit and truth."

²⁵The woman said to Him, "I know that Messiah is coming" (who is called Christ). "When He comes, He will tell us all things."

²⁶Jesus said to her, "I who speak to you am He."

John 4:23-26

Have you ever had the feeling of being stuck in the bottom of a dark, dank well? Maybe circumstances threw you in, or maybe you jumped in of your own volition. I can truthfully say that both of the above are included in the storyline of my life. How refreshing it is to splash in the living water of God's grace. The longer you've been barely afloat in the dormant water at the bottom of the well, the sweeter it is when you rise above it. The discovery of who you truly are in Christ Jesus is fascinating and exhilarating!

At thirty-five years old, I discovered that I was not just a somebody to God but a somebody worth loving! God slowly began to peel away the layers of lies of an abusive earthly father. All my life, the lies of being unlovable were buried deep inside my heart. God patiently and lovingly carried me down the path to spiritual change where I accepted His love for me. It was not altogether a pretty or easy road to travel, but my loving and patient heavenly Father thought I was worth the journey. At fifty-two, I live to serve Him and spread His love to others.

~ Anonymous

Oh, yes, my friend, our Lord is all about drawing us deeply into His love. Just as this abusive earthly father heaped on lies of unworthiness, the enemy heaps on lies that your life is merely ordinary and will amount to nothing special. But God longs to create *extraordinary* out of your *ordinary*! It's your choice, however. He will never force extraordinary on you, but He hopes you'll choose it. I'd like to explore this topic with you today; but first, here's something for you to think

132   *Anonymous*

about and give your response. Remember, anything goes. When I ask for your thoughts, then whatever you reply is merely what you're thinking. There's no right or wrong answer.

Why do you think many Christians feel ordinary when the extraordinary God lives inside of them?

I've been there, in that place of ordinary, and most probably you have been, too. Let's take a look at the Scriptures and explore this topic of being extraordinary in Christ. Here's my thinking: if extraordinary is possible, I want it! How about you?

Fill in the blanks as you look at John 4:23 in today's Scripture.

Jesus said that _____ worshipers will worship the Father in _____ and _____.

What do you consider to be characteristics of a true worshiper?

This phrase tells us that true worshipers are those who are not worshiping in name only. They do not simply give the resemblance of worship but are genuine in their worship. And where is true worship determined—where does it take place? In spirit, that connection between the believer and God. It's about the state of mind and heart in which we worship Him. A true worship experience is not only about the object of worship but also the nature of worship. As Jesus spoke to her, He wanted her to know that the consummation of these truths was at hand. Perhaps He also wanted her to have this information to draw upon later, when she heard of His crucifixion and resurrection.

Let's keep going by unpacking the phrase *worship in spirit and truth*. The best way I can illustrate this expression is with a personal example. I think of it as a mergence of the physical with the spiritual realm. It's what happens when I share a sweet time with my heavenly Father in worship on most mornings. As intimate moments go, it's rather private, but I'm glad to share with you because I believe it will give understanding to our thoughts on worship.

Soon after I awaken in the mornings, I enjoy getting on my knees before the Father with an offering of myself for the day ahead. As best I can, I imagine what the day holds as I talk over Romans 12:1 with Him. My prayer may go something like this:

Father, You've looked my way and drawn me to You, so it's by Your mercies that I present to You my body, mind, and emotions for the day before me. Lord, I give You every thought and feeling as a living sacrifice, holy and acceptable to You. If there are negative feelings, I offer them to You. If things go well, they belong to You too. After all You've done and are doing for me, it's only reasonable that I make this offering. May it be holy and acceptable to You.

As I continue worshiping with His Word and giving the run-down of my day, I specifically talk through the details with Him. *Worshiping in spirit and truth* in this context means that I connect with God, spirit to Spirit. Although I do not literally sacrifice my life in the physical sense, I truly do sacrifice my life in the spiritual realm, offering everything to God. My worship is sincere, genuine, and from my heart. That's how I know it's pleasing to God as I worship Him in this way.

Though your worship will be unique to you, as it should be, your connection with God also should be genuine and complete—holding nothing back.

My friend, if you are feeling trapped in the *ordinary*, you can break free by joining with Jesus and moving in agreement with His Spirit of Truth who says any moment of any day is *extraordinary* when lived in Him! If Jesus lives inside of You, your salvation is a done deal. But if you are going to live victoriously in this life, you have to make the choice to do so. I believe that choice involves worshiping Him in spirit and in truth. Let's take this illustration a bit deeper.

Earthbound living presents you with many opportunities to choose what you will think and how you will respond. Let's say you're in a situation where you feel shunned, overlooked, underappreciated, of no value—well, you get the picture. Your mind starts processing and sending messages to your emotions. You have options of what to believe. I'll list some:

Nobody thinks I'm important.	*I'm lower than low.*
Just wait; one day they'll notice.	*I'm embarrassed to even be here.*
I hate being around people.	*Nobody wants to be with me.*

These are some typical messages the mind sends. You, my friend, are not your thoughts but the chooser of your thoughts. Knowing that the extraordinary God lives inside you, you can choose His thoughts over the thoughts that first pop into your mind when you are dismissed by others. Here's an example: *I don't feel very valued right now, but I know You value me Lord. Thank You.*

Now it's your turn. Write three "God's Thoughts" statements that connect with your current emotions.

1.

2.

3.

One of my all-time favorite strategies is to begin thanking God when uncomfortable or exceptionally ordinary moments in life hit.

Thank You, Lord, that You are giving me opportunity right now to focus on the Truth living inside of me. Although I'm really uncomfortable/discouraged in this situation, I am one with You. You love me and have chosen me to live life with You. I worship You in this Truth. May this moment bring You glory.

You can, by choice, turn unpleasant times into worship times by offering them to your heavenly Father.

Record the physical description of Jesus found in Isaiah 53:2.

According to this verse, in what way was Jesus ordinary?

Now think of your own life—who you are, what you do. Do you consider yourself to be exceptional or rather common? How does the representation of Jesus in this verse impact your thoughts about what you consider to be ordinary about you and your life?

Think about this for just a moment: are you willing to accept every moment of every day that your heavenly Father has provided for you—even if there are moments ahead that leave you feeling ordinary, overlooked, and unnoticed?

In Philippians 4:12, the apostle Paul wrote these words:

> *I know how to be abased, and I know how to abound. Everywhere and in all things I have learned both to be full and to be hungry, both to abound and to suffer need.*

Look up the word *abased* in a print or online dictionary, and write the definition below:

For me, some of the most precious worship times I've enjoyed have been during earthly episodes of feeling overlooked, very ordinary, and unvalued. It's during such times that Christ longs to grow His humility within us. He will give us deep perspective into His heart when we cease to find our value in earthly relationships and circumstances.

My sister, are you like the woman at the well? Are you longing for the day when you'll meet the Messiah and find your answers to life's difficulties and perplexities in Him? Do you want something magnificent in your commonplace living? I tenderly implore you to realize that He's here for you in the *now* of your life. This very moment you can hear Him say, "I who speak to you am *He*" (John 4:26).

You don't have to wait until perfection in heaven to experience victory! Sure, you'll be completely victorious then, but you can experience much of it now. Hear Him speaking as He draws You into His heart of love. Nothing escapes the loving and sovereign eye of the Lord, and He is always looking at your heart of worship. As you make it a practice to worship God in spirit and truth, you'll begin to experience excitement that exceeds the earthly kind. Your passion to bring glory to God in worshiping Him will refresh your own spirit. This kind of satisfaction will fulfill your very being. That's the way He designed it.

Take a few moments right now to talk with your heavenly Father. What is He speaking to you in today's lesson? Write some thoughts below.

Today's Touchpoint

Read John 4:27-34. Allow your mind to visualize the conclusion of this wonderful story recorded for us in God's Word. I like to imagine the looks on the disciples' faces when they returned and found Jesus in conversation with the Samaritan woman. I can see them offering Him food and urging Him to eat.

What was Jesus' reply to them in verse 32?

What do you think He meant?

It makes me smile to think of them questioning each other, "Has anyone brought Him *anything* to eat?" (John 4:33).

Especially intriguing to me is the behavior of our woman of the week. From our Scripture passage, there are many awesome things we know that she and Jesus talked about: living water, the fountain of water springing up into everlasting life, religious practices, salvation, worshiping in spirit and truth, along with the coming of the Messiah. In light of the holy things they talked about, take a look at verse 29:

> *"Come, see a Man who told me all things that I ever did. Could this be the*
> *Christ?"*

In this awesome conversation, what astonished her the most? She marveled at the fact that Jesus *knew her!* I'm sure when she realized "Jesus knows me, this I love," it soon gave birth to "Jesus loves me, this I know." How wonderful it is to know that our extraordinary God knows us ordinary women!

Oh, my friends, may the fact that Jesus knows us and knows everything about us create the same kind of awe, wonder, and love in our hearts. *Yes, indeed, He truly is the Christ!*

Oh, one more question: Did she ever give Him that drink of water? You decide!

Dear Father, thank You for knowing me. Thank You for revealing Your Word to my heart and mind this week. Teach me to walk boldly and unashamedly in Your truth and in Your love. I love You so. Amen.

Week 4
Video Viewer Guide

• • • • • • • • • • • • • • • • • •

[Jesus] left Judea and departed again to Galilee. But He needed to go through Samaria.

John 4:3-4 NKJV

He _____ to go through Samaria.

So He came to a city of Samaria which is called Sychar. . . . Now Jacob's well was there. Jesus therefore, being wearied from His journey, sat thus by the well.

John 4:5-6 NKJV

Jesus was _____.

A woman of Samaria came to draw water.
John 4:7a NKJV

Jesus said to her, "Give Me a _____."
John 4:7b NKJV

You will _____ God to the degree that you know God enjoys

_____.

If you are not having an active, engaging, exciting relationship with Jesus Christ, . . .

how much does it _____ to you?

Determine with God in the beginning of the day to _____ for Him and see

Him in _____ places.

Week 5

The Woman Who Committed Adultery

When You Are Burdened with Shame

Her Story

2 Now early in the morning He came again into the temple, and all the people came to Him; and He sat down and taught them. 3 Then the scribes and Pharisees brought to Him a woman caught in adultery. And when they had set her in the midst, 4 they said to Him, "Teacher, this woman was caught in adultery, in the very act. 5 Now Moses, in the law, commanded us that such should be stoned. But what do You say?" 6 This they said, testing Him, that they might have something of which to accuse Him. But Jesus stooped down and wrote on the ground with His finger, as though He did not hear.

7 So when they continued asking Him, He raised Himself up and said to them, "He who is without sin among you, let him throw a stone at her first." 8 And again He stooped down and wrote on the ground. 9 Then those who heard it, being convicted by their conscience, went out one by one, beginning with the oldest even to the last. And Jesus was left alone, and the woman standing in the midst. 10 When Jesus had raised Himself up and saw no one but the woman, He said to her, "Woman, where are those accusers of yours? Has no one condemned you?"

11 She said, "No one, Lord."

And Jesus said to her, "Neither do I condemn you; go and sin no more."

12 Then Jesus spoke to them again, saying, "I am the light of the world. He who follows Me shall not walk in darkness, but have the light of life."

John 8:2-12

Her Name: *Shame*

The title for this week's study gets your attention, right? Honestly, I wanted to go with another title, but to keep in harmony with the headings of our content, it was necessary to refer to her as *the woman who comitted adultery*. Her nameless label follows suit with the previous ones—*the woman who anointed Jesus, the woman with the issue of blood*, and *the woman at the well*. So, like the others, that's how we've come to know her.

My hesitancy with the label is that some may place greater emphasis on the sin rather than on God's grace. But alas, the sin is a huge part of the grace. Because that's true, I'm tremendously excited about this week's content. I've anticipated getting here to unwrap and unpack God's incredible Word concerning the divine and mysterious reality of His heart of forgiveness.

As I've said before, I'm getting so close to these women we're studying. It's like they've become part of our girlfriend study group. I hope your experience is the same as you've gathered together to discuss their lives and the dilemmas they faced. More than before, I'm seeing them as real flesh and blood women facing the same types of situations we face today. Of course, there are distinguishing characteristics brought on by culture, lifestyle, and a couple of thousand years; but the emotions and what I call the "woman response factor" are much the same. Do you agree?

With those thoughts in play, as I launched into researching John 8, my mind recalled a scene from years ago. I was sitting at my kitchen counter, weeping over an issue that had left me with a raw heart interlaced with raveled emotions. God spoke to me in that moment, as He's apt to do when every other voice is muddled and nonsensical.

What if the worst thing that ever happened to you is really the best thing?

I replied, "How could that be, Lord?" And immediately I knew. The worst brought me to the Best. The awful carried me to the Glorious. It always does if we so allow.

My friend, you have a worst, don't you? Everyone does. It may involve something you have done or something that's been done to you. Your worst thing truly can be your best thing. With our three previous women from Scripture, we've seen how their encounters with Jesus made this statement reality for each of them. Their sin, suffering, and status in life brought them straight to the Lord. Will you allow yours to do the same?

We don't know all the particulars of the adulterous woman's tangled web, but we do know how God's grace brought her to the most wonderful person of all, Jesus Christ. And in understanding her journey, our own is impacted. Whether we need to be forgiven or to practice forgiveness, the scene that unfolds in John 8 with these law-mongers, the accused one, and Jesus, will show us how to deal with shame, judgment, and restoration. Get pumped—there's an exciting and freeing week ahead!

I'm praying for His best for you!

Memory Verse

Therefore, if anyone is in Christ, [she] is a new creation; old things have passed away; behold, all things have become new.

2 Corinthians 5:17

Take it to heart my friend—for yourself and for those in Christ around you. Study it. Memorize it. Rejoice over it.

Day 1: The Trap

Focus: Annihilating Shame

Scripture:

³Then the scribes and Pharisees brought to Him a woman caught in adultery. And when they had set her in the midst, ⁴they said to Him, "Teacher, this woman was caught in adultery, in the very act. ⁵Now Moses, in the law, commanded us that such should be stoned. But what do You say?"

John 8:3-5

To begin with, let's take a look at the accusers in this dramatic encounter with Jesus—the scribes and the Pharisees. For the most part, they were adversaries of Jesus during His life on earth. Being well-versed legal experts who could draft legal documents involving money, marriage, land ownership, and so forth, these men were also knowledgeable about Jewish law and tradition. This being true, they certainly had a legal eye on Jesus.

But when the Pharisees saw this, they said to his disciples, "Why does your teacher eat with tax collectors and sinners?" (Matthew 9:11 CEB)

And when the scribes and Pharisees saw Him eating with the tax collectors and sinners, they said to His disciples, "How is it that He eats and drinks with tax collectors and sinners?" (Mark 2:16)

The legal experts came down from Jerusalem. Over and over they charged, "He's possessed by Beelzebul. He throws out demons with the authority of the ruler of demons." (Mark 3:22 CEB)

Read the verses above and answer the following questions:

What did the Pharisees ask the disciples in Matthew 9:11?

What were the Pharisees saying about Jesus through the question they asked in Mark 2:16?

What did they say about Him in Mark 3:22, and what was their reasoning?

In reading the Gospel accounts, it's apparent these enemies of Jesus were very zealous in challenging His behavior and teaching. The way Jesus interpreted the law not only caught them off guard, it struck at the very core of who they were. These religious purists emphasized methods and strict adherence to *their* interpretation of the Mosaic law. What about Jesus and His attitude toward the Pharisees?

Read Matthew 23:13-36 and summarize in your own words what Jesus thought about such legalism:

In my Bible study *Desperate* (LifeWay 2012), I describe this rules-and-regulations mentality in this way:

> If nothing else, the Pharisees were masters of law complication and manipulation. For example, God simply said, "Remember the Sabbath day by keeping it holy" (Exodus 20:8, NIV). Members of this Jewish sect of strict law-keepers were so afraid of earning God's wrath that they took that commandment and came up with over 600 regulations regarding Sabbath keeping. While we may respect their intentions, we would probably agree that many of these laws were ridiculously strict. For instance, one Sabbath law forbade a woman to pick up a needle that she dropped on the floor. The reason? If she picked it up, it might accidentally scratch the dirt floor which would be too much like plowing a field.
>
> Such legalities have a problem. While they may appear to be about honoring God, they produce hollow obedience based on outside actions without any connection to the heart. In fact, such strictness actually creates distance from God rather than intimacy with Him.[1]

Do you think your behavior this past Sunday (our holy day of rest as Christians) would have passed the pharisaical law-keeping code? I know mine wouldn't.

This group, generally speaking, operated outside of compassion. They taught about God, but they didn't seem to love God. Being overly concerned with externals, they neglected the real and simple truth about God and His relationship with humankind. So blinded by their observances and nitpicky details, they completely missed the Messiah in their midst.

Turn to Mark 7:6-7. What words from the prophet Isaiah did Jesus use to describe the hypocrisy of the Pharisees?

Now, let's take a look at the particular crime of adultery. The Jewish law declared that marital unfaithfulness was punishable by stoning. The Old Testament listed it as a capital crime, according to Leviticus 20:10 (HCSB):

If a man commits adultery with a married woman—if he commits adultery with his neighbor's wife—both the adulterer and the adulteress must be put to death.

According to this verse, *who* must be put to death?

Now read Deuteronomy 22:22 below. Who shall die, according to this law?

Who was brought to Jesus in John 8:3?

———————————

"If a man is found lying with a woman married to a husband, then both of them shall die—the man that lay with the woman, and the woman; so you shall put away the evil from Israel. (Deuteronomy 22:22)

———————————

Of course, the obvious question is, *Where was the man?*

● ● ● ● ● ●

Take a quick review of what we've already discussed today, along with the Scripture references we've looked at. What is your take on why only the woman was brought to Jesus? Write your thoughts below.

Before we can really appreciate how this passage unfolds, it's important to get a grasp on those involved and the background of this setting. This will help give understanding to the comment that Jesus makes later when He addresses the accusers.

In addition to the issue of only the woman being brought to Jesus, there's another matter to consider. These sticklers of the law knew what was mandated by the law. Why, then, did they ask Jesus His opinion? At the outset, it sounds like an honest request for justice, doesn't it? "Teacher, this woman was caught in adultery, in the very act. Now Moses, in the law, commanded us that such should be stoned. But what do You say?"(John 8:4-5).

But we must remember that these law keepers did not believe Jesus to be the Messiah. Their intent in this matter was not to deliver justice, for they could have done that apart from Jesus. It appears a clever trap was what they had in mind; they wanted to discredit Jesus along with His teaching. Yep, they were setting Him up.

Let's review the facts so far:

- The scribes and Pharisees presented to Jesus a woman that they had *caught in the act*.
- Theirs was an airtight case, they thought, intended to trap Him.
- If Jesus answered, "Stone her," He would prove inconsistent with His teaching and behavior since He was a friend to sinners. If He answered, "Let her go," He would appear to be an enemy of the law of Moses and a condoner of sin.

Little did they know, Jesus had it all covered!

Now, let's take these verses and "download" them into your mind and heart. I want to stimulate your thinking a bit by leading you to consider the three viewpoints presented in this passage.

First, take a look at the situation through the eyes of the Pharisees. Their interest was in dealing with people who broke the law. Their typical *modus operandi* (method of operation) was that the offender should receive justice; justice should be allowed to run its course. They laid out the law, along with their duty to implement it. This approach, itself, sounds rather noble. Remember the loophole of the missing man along with the underlying plot to trap Jesus.

Can you think of a time when a hard-line approach to doing things right caused you or another to dismiss compassion? Include in your thoughts areas outside the legal system. Make some notes below.

Second, take a look through the eyes of *Shame*. She is not a fictional character in some clandestine romance novel. She was a real flesh and blood soul who was surely humiliated, mortified, and shamed beyond expression. Could this have been some flagrant scandal that was ingeniously contrived with the sole purpose of discrediting Jesus? Had she even been solicited as the centerpiece of this ploy?

Have you or someone you know ever been publicly shamed? If so, share a few thoughts, if you're willing.

My heartache for this woman at this moment in her storyline is intense, so I quickly move forward to the reality of her worst becoming her best—which brings us to Jesus.

Finally, take a look at the situation through Jesus' pure eyes that see 100 percent sin alongside 100 percent grace. As I look through the eyes of Jesus, I become spiritually spellbound by His love. I am captivated by His response to her heart, and I am thrilled that He speaks the same to mine—and to yours.

For all have sinned and fall short of the glory of God. (Romans 3:23)

For the wages of sin is death, but the gift of God is eternal life in Christ Jesus our Lord. (Romans 6:23)

Write Romans 3:23 in your own words:

According to Romans 6:23, what do we deserve?

Now turn to John 8:10-11, the end of this righteous showdown, and record the words of Jesus to this scornful woman:

We'll explore this statement of Jesus later in the week, but for now hear me shout, "Holy hallelujah!" This divine drama shows how Jesus stands up for sinners in the face of the law. We, the sinner woman, stand condemned under the law before God. He Who detests sin loves the sinner. Grace takes on what rightfully belongs to us—the proclamation of sin and death. His love sends us on our way with the charge "sin no more."

Our proper response? Heartfelt gratitude for His mercy and love, committing ourselves—with His help—to sin no more.

Today's Touchpoint

What an honor it is to bring you before our Lord at the conclusion of each day's lesson. As *Anonymous* Bible study girlfriends, I like to think of us sitting across from each other enjoying conversation over coffee or tea. Often I "sit" with girlfriends I've made through ministry by reading e-mails. I love to hear how God is working in other women's lives. These accounts of faith strengthen me and cause me to rejoice in our God. Perhaps you do the same—in person and through e-mail and social media—with the girlfriends you've made through Bible study. Yes, God has given us girlfriends so that in each other we may find comfort, encouragement, and joy in His presence.

So, my girlfriend, I have a pertinent question for you. Is there *a something* in your recent or distant past that you flat out long to erase? If so, you are joining the ranks of many who have often recoiled at the flashbacks that run across their mental display screens. Aren't memories supposed to fade with the passing of time? If the picture of your forgiven sin is not fading, there's your first clue that something's amiss in your thinking. It's a tactic of the enemy of our souls to keep these images streaming across our minds.

Below, write Micah 7:19 and include today's date beside it.

On our own, our sin and the anguish it creates is simply too hard for us to handle. But if Jesus lives inside of us, He has taken this sin away. He has broken the power of sin so that it may not have dominion over us.

Is it possible to be free but still experience guilt? Absolutely! It's not God's plan for us to do so, but many do just the same. The question is asked in a favorite hymn from long ago: "Would you be free from the *burden* of sin?"[2] My friend, if you have been freed from sin, you've also been freed from the *burden* of that sin and its hold on you.

Psalm 55:22a in the Amplified Bible calls us to "Cast your burden on the Lord [releasing the weight of it] and He will sustain you." Though this verse pertains to any burden, I'd like you to think of it specifically in regards to the burden of sin.

Follow the counsel of Psalm 55:22 by writing a prayer request to the Lord, specifically casting the burden of sin upon Him. Place today's date beside your hand-written prayer.

Stick with me. What I'm asking you to do may seem a bit far-fetched to some, but I'd like for you to give it a try. Imagine the three of us (Jesus, you, and me) in conversation together, discussing this burden of sin issue. Imagine the smile on our Lord's face as you accept His grace and honor Him by releasing your burden.

Dear Lord, I have been dragged by the accuser to the best possible place, Your presence! Thank You that I now stand before You cleansed, refreshed, and free from sin and its burden. Teach me how to honor You each time that burden tries to take up residence in my heart and mind. As many times as it takes, give me the fortitude to lay down what You've already dealt with by dying on the cross to save me from this sin. Thank You—more than I can express. I love You. Amen.

Day 2: The Seriousness of Sin and the Wideness of God's Grace

Focus: The Unfolding of Grace

Scripture:

⁶This they said, testing Him, that they might have something of which to accuse Him. But Jesus stooped down and wrote on the ground with His finger, as though He did not hear.

⁷So when they continued asking Him, He raised Himself up and said to them, "He who is without sin among you, let him throw a stone at her first."

John 8:6-7

Yesterday we set the tone for God's grace. Our study, backed by Scripture, made it clear that God has covered every one of our sins, including adultery, by His blood shed on the cross. While it's essential that we always accept the gracious forgiveness of our Lord, it's also important that we acknowledge the gravity of an adulterous situation. The breach of physical and emotional intimacy between spouses grieves the heart of God and mocks the holy union that He has ordained between husband and wife. God does not intend for this union to be broken except in death. According to the words of Jesus in Matthew 19:9, He sees the breach of adultery as such a serious grievance that it is grounds for divorce.

There's awesome news, however. If you have been affected in some way by the sin of adultery, know that God's forgiveness has you covered. God's grace attends you. My friend, you may stand as the one accused, or you may be the victim of the emotional and mental fallout that accompanies the situation. Either way, God's great love covers all who are involved and touched by this far-reaching sin.

Read 1 John 1:9 (see next page). What assurance do we find in this verse?

Now read Matthew 6:14 (below). Why is it important for us to forgive others?

_____

If we confess our sins, He is faithful and just to forgive us our sins and to cleanse us from all unrighteousness. (1 John 1:9)

For if you forgive other people when they sin against you, your heavenly Father will also forgive you. (Matthew 6:14 NIV)

_____

Emotional healing takes time, determination, and the willingness to receive and extend God's forgiveness and grace. In fact, receiving and extending forgiveness and grace are the only ways to cleanse and close the deep wounds gouged into the soul by infidelity. Reconciliation is possible only when both parties are willing to do the hard work involved. And there are those times when reconciliation is simply not advisable. Either way, healing *can* take place—when there is reconciliation and also when there is not. Forgiveness and reconciliation are two separate things. It is possible to forgive yet choose not to reconcile. For instance, the anonymous sister who shared the story below does not state whether or not her marriage was restored. Either way, when we come to God with genuine repentance for our sin, His grace always abounds.

> *For several years, I was this woman. Never would I have imagined this life for me. I knew it was wrong, but when I became one held captive to immorality, I began to rationalize. "If this is so wrong, God, why did you let it happen to me?" Well, He didn't "make" it happen, but He allowed me to make choices. And I made one wrong choice after another. Eventually I found myself in a horrid pit. God never stopped pursuing me, though, even while I was sinning against Him.*
>
> *This is the truth recorded in Psalm 40:2-3 (NASB): "He brought me up out of the pit of destruction, out of the miry clay, / And He set my feet upon a rock making my footsteps firm. / He put a new song in my mouth, a song of praise to our God." Jesus Christ is my Rock. He washed me clean through the power of His blood, forgave my sin, and made me a new creation in Christ! He took away my shame and guilt and gave me a brand new beginning.*
>
> *~Anonymous*

What a beautiful testimony of a life restored in Jesus Christ! Thankfully, this sister made the determined choice to climb out of that sin-pit with God's strength. Being a recipient of His grace, she goes on to say, is the very thing that gave her new life and freedom from guilt.

Read Hebrews 8:12 (below). What does God specifically say about recalling our sins?

God's healing is ushered in through confession and repentance of our sins. He not only "remembers them no more," He also lavishes His balm of healing to the wounded soul.

"For I will forgive their wickedness / and will remember their sins no more."
(Hebrews 8:12 NIV)

I thought my life was over when I realized my husband had been unfaithful to me. I thought we had a wonderful marriage, so this news punched me in the gut. His confession to me was difficult to hear. He was a broken man asking for forgiveness. I never thought I'd be called to practice God's love in this way. We both knew as Christians that a divorce was permissible by God's Word for adultery. We chose instead to lean on the Lord and heal our marriage. That's been many years ago, and I'm encouraged to testify of God's faithfulness to heal when we practice His love.

~ Anonymous

It's so wonderfully exhilarating to see the story of God's redemption played out in restored marriages. Though many relationships are not restored after infidelity, I am so thankful for stories of encouragement like this, shared from the hearts of those who have been deeply wounded by sin. Yet even when a couple does not reconcile, the beautiful truth is that God's grace still abounds. God is always at work, forgiving sin and bringing healing and restoration wherever it is needed.

If you have not experienced the hurt of infidelity firsthand, it is likely that you or someone you love has been affected by it. It is critical to remember that while the ripple effects of the sin of adultery can affect family, friendships, and community, *nothing* is beyond God's forgiveness. In fact, I've seen God work miraculously to restore hearts in such experiences. As with every other sin, God through His redemptive work on the cross brings healing and joy. It becomes all about Him and His grace.

Pause for a few moments of reflection. What is the Holy Spirit speaking to your heart right now? Write some thoughts in the space below or in a journal.

We certainly see both the seriousness of sin and the wideness of God's grace in the story of the woman who committed adultery. As I mentioned yesterday, the Pharisees were hoping to ensnare Jesus in His speech. These accusers addressed Him with the law of Moses as their backdrop. They planned for His verbal reply to their questioning to be the rope that would hang Him. Surely He wouldn't go against the holy law of Moses, right?

The next sequence in this sacred drama is rather mystifying. It's also one of my favorite word pictures in all of Scripture. I'm caught up in how it unfolds. I'm also intrigued by the fact that we are invited to use our God-given imaginations to fancy the message of Jesus as He stoops down and writes:

> *But Jesus stooped down and wrote on the ground with His finger, as though He did not hear.*

John 8:6b

Was Jesus stalling for time? Though some have suggested that possibility, my heartfelt response is "Gracious no!" I side with those scholars who point out that Jesus was never caught off guard by questions or the tests of others.

Why do you think Jesus behaved as though He did not hear?

What do you think those hoping to indict Him thought of His silence?

Silence is a powerful form of communication. It's not only the absence of sound but also the conveyor of great meaning. Silence can be perceived as negative or positive. During personal periods of silence, I've experienced conviction of sin, fresh insights, recalling of random facts, and divine direction. I've also experienced feelings that left me uncomfortable, energized, and motivated. And I confess that sometimes I enjoy the reaction of the one receiving my silence!

Recall a negative experience of silence and a positive experience of silence. Describe each.

Negative experience:

Positive experience:

Depending on your state of mind and the situation, it's easy to jump to conclusions during a quiet lull in conversation. Maybe the Pharisees were thinking, *We've got Him this time. He doesn't know how to answer.* Or this silence could have panicked them, leaving them to wonder about His next move.

Whether they were emboldened or they lost their nerve, they pressed in. With their continual questioning, Jesus rose from where He had stooped on the ground. Then, He dropped this verbal bomb:

> *"He who is without sin among you, let him throw a stone at her first."*
> John 8:7b

Come on, girls, isn't this one of the greatest lines in all of Scripture? Jesus neither addressed the law nor excused her guilt. He merely turned the sentencing back on them, silencing them to shame with this infamous, holy one-liner.

In your own words, tell what you think Jesus meant by this statement.

I smile thinking of how our new girlfriend *Shame* must have taken this news upon hearing the words of Jesus. We aren't told, but we can certainly imagine. What do you think?

Let your imagination roll and list some possible thoughts that this real woman might have had:

It was with great spiritual finesse that Jesus resolved the case and broke the snare. His actions provide us with a godly plumb line for those times when altercations are close at hand. Silence can be a great advocator, and taking time to think is always to our advantage.

Let's circle back now and take a closer look at what Jesus did during those moments of silence, before delivering his brilliant one-liner. This is my favorite part of the story. *What did Jesus write on the ground?*

I've long been fascinated by this portion of John 8. As I read about the Pharisees questioning Jesus, I envision the face of our Lord remaining calm and nonaccusing, even knowing they were walking Him into a trap.

Yesterday we looked at other occasions when Jesus spoke sternly to the Pharisees concerning their hypocrisy. But because He loved all people and was known for giving sinners a second chance, we know that He still loved them and longed for them to open their hearts to Him, just as Nicodemus did (see John 3). So in my mental replaying of this scene, I see the humility and graciousness of our Lord at work as He stoops to write.

Let me ask some questions to jumpstart your thinking about this message Jesus wrote on the ground. *Scripture gives us no answers to these questions.* Simply jot down your own thoughts and speculations, or let these questions lead you to write other questions of your own.

To whom was Jesus writing?

Did He write something from Scripture? Something else?

Did his writing have to do with the law, with grace, or with both?

Were the accusers convicted by His written word(s)?

Did the accused woman find comfort in what He wrote?

This is the only account in the Gospels that mentions Jesus writing. That really intrigues me. I love God's Word, and I get a kick out of imagining what might fill the "blanks" left in the stories I read. I even asked the Lord what He wrote on the ground that day, and though He didn't tell me (and I didn't think He would), He filled my heart with a quizzical hunger to know more about the way He loves. Believing my curiosity will be satisfied one day, I've placed this question on my future "Ask Jesus List."

Whatever Jesus wrote in the dirt, there's one thing we know for certain because of what happened next: His grace was wide enough to encompass all who were watching and waiting. And His grace is wide enough still!

Today's Touchpoint

My friend, this story touches upon some rather heavy content, doesn't it? Sometimes our stories do as well. But as God's children we can always choose to celebrate the goodness of our Lord. Even during the rough, tough, dismal days of earthly living, He is still victorious on His throne. And if we're in Him, then so are we!

It has been several years ago, but the sweet freshness of the moment bursts anew in my heart each time I recall it. I was considering the things that just hadn't worked out the way I'd planned and dreamed. As I was mulling this over early one morning, I heard God's voice speaking directly to my spirit. He said, "What if everything you've ever dreamed of and hoped for came true—how would you be celebrating?"

I smiled as I imagined myself dancing and giggling over these dreams come true. He spoke again to my spirit, "Well, do it!" Immediately the translation to my spirit was, "Celebrate simply because I'm God!"

So, I did! You can make that same choice right now. Because of Him, there's always reason to celebrate! Take some time to do this now. May our Lord fill your heart with joy as you celebrate who you are in Him—for this moment and forever more!

Dear heavenly Father, right now I choose to celebrate Who You are! I celebrate Your faithfulness and Your grace. Thank You for Your Word, which encourages me and spurs me on to heavenly thinking. I love how You draw me into the lives of those I read about in Scripture. Thank You for giving us this picture of true love and grace in John 8. Thank You for Christian girlfriends, and for being the best Friend of all. I love You. Amen.

Day 3: Spiritual Showdown

Focus: Seeing into the Heart

Scripture:

[7]So when they continued asking Him, He raised Himself up and said to them, "He who is without sin among you, let him throw a stone at her first."

[8]And again He stooped down and wrote on the ground. [9]Then those who heard it, being convicted by their conscience, went out one by one, beginning with the oldest even to the last. And Jesus was left alone, and the woman standing in the midst.

John 8:7-9

Are you noticing the twists and turns in the plot of this unfolding storyline? All of a sudden, suspicion shifts from the woman to this band of finger-pointers. With subtle ease, Jesus turns the conviction of the one accused upon the ones accusing. His words—perhaps in combination with whatever He wrote on the ground—were the impetus that prompted the retreat of the Pharisees.

Yesterday we looked at verse 6 and saw that as Jesus was writing, he acted "as though He did not hear." My impression as this conspiracy unravels is that they gradually realized He not only heard their *spoken* words but also the *unspoken* ones in their hearts.

Now, let's explore another intriguing nuance in the shifting of focus from the woman who was accused to those who were accusing.

Take another look at John 8:8-9 and fill in the blanks:

Jesus stooped down and _____ on the ground.

Those who _____ it went out one by one.

What the Pharisees heard audibly was Jesus' comment, "He who is without sin among you, let Him throw a stone at her first." There's no doubt that this comment affected their response. But once again I'd like to challenge you to step out of the box and use your God-given imagination.

Is it possible that what Jesus wrote affected their behavior as well? In verse 8 we read that Jesus *wrote*, and then in verse 9 we read that they *heard*. Perhaps they "heard" more than what Jesus said aloud.

Is it possible to hear when no words are spoken? In Revelation 2:7 we read, "He who has an ear, let him hear what the Spirit says." With the Holy Spirit living inside of us, we have a discerning spiritual "ear," an ear of understanding. Yesterday I described how God spoke to my spirit about celebrating. I call this the audible, inaudible voice of God. It is audible to my spirit even though it is inaudible to the ears.

Have you ever heard the *audible, inaudible* voice of God speaking to your spirit? If so, write about the experience. (Choose a recent or memorable experience.)

Now, at the time of this biblical encounter, the Holy Spirit had not yet been sent by the Father. But I believe that having Jesus in their midst evidently opened their spiritual ears to hear a word from Him. Having just thunderstruck them with the words, "He who is without sin among you, let him throw a stone at her first" (v. 7b), Jesus then paused again and stooped to the ground to continue writing.

Oh, the gravity of that moment must have weighed heavily on their hearts and minds! They did not hear *silence*; they heard *conviction*. The text tells us, "Then those who heard it, being convicted by their conscience, went out one by one, beginning with the oldest even to the last" (v. 9). I believe Jesus was speaking to their hearts and they were hearing.

Let's do a little "heart talk."

Turn to Jeremiah 17. How does the prophet Jeremiah describe the heart in verse 9?

According to verse 10, who searches the heart and tests the mind?

In verse 1, where do we learn Judah's sin is written?

Now read Matthew 15:19 (below). What comes from the heart?

_____

Out of the heart come evil thoughts, murders, adultery, sexual sins, thefts, false testimonies, and insults. (Matthew 15:19 CEB)

_____

We live in a time in which popular counsel advises, "Be true to your heart. Follow your heart. Listen to the leanings of your heart."

Scripturally speaking, why is this poor advice?

Do you think there's ever a time you can trust your heart? Explain your answer.

Given the description of how the Pharisees departed the scene, I'd say the words of Jesus about throwing stones got lodged in their hearts. I wonder how many times these individuals replayed that shocking line. I wonder if each time they did, they felt a check in their spirit—if not a boulder in their gut. Whether it was the words spoken to the physical ear or those spoken to the spiritual ear, something caused these men to stop persecuting Jesus and to stop prosecuting the woman.

Perhaps along with their conviction, they were frightened of their motives being discovered. Or maybe it was the combination of the two that led them to disappear into the crowd one by one. The conscience is a powerful communicator of God's truth. Given the way they pulled away, could they have possibly felt shame over the whole ordeal?

Since this particular incident is not followed up with scriptural details, we're left to wonder what happened next. Did some of them return to Jesus after His dealings with the woman? I like to think that what happened in their hearts during this quiet confrontation gave some of them reason enough to investigate His claims of being the Messiah. We must remember that Christ's design for

grace is for everyone. I believe that Jesus sought to lovingly bring the woman to repentance as He strategically and silently revealed the sins of the men who brought her there.

Now we come to a powerful sentence in the story that creates a beautiful word picture for us:

And Jesus was left alone, and the woman standing in the midst. (v. 9b)

This word picture will set the stage for our study tomorrow—the moment when grace meets sin. For now, I just want us to linger here and let this word picture become a still frame in our hearts.

Back up to John 8:2. Reading that verse as the backdrop to our still frame, how would you describe the setting?

Here's my visual of this one moment. I see Jesus writing from His kneeling position. In the background are people milling around, with a few glancing toward Him. Between them, I see a trembling woman with a rather disheveled appearance. With this as our mental landscape, let's consider Jesus first and then the woman called *Shame*.

The words "And Jesus was left alone" tug at my heart. We must remember that even though He was fully God, He also was fully man. Jesus was no emotional wimp, but He was so tender within His humanness. I believe that He was hopeful those accusers would come to Him instead of go away from Him. But one by one, they chose to go away.

The accusers had a critical choice at the moment of their conviction, just as you and I do at the moment of ours. What is that choice?

Recall a time when you chose to turn to Jesus when you felt conviction. Describe the experience.

As I've meditated on John 8:9, a fresh awareness has hit me about the *aloneness* of Jesus. Though often surrounded by a crowd, Jesus also was frequently left alone. In fact, we read in Scripture that Jesus often withdrew from the crowd to rest or pray. Though generally we see this in a positive light, as a good and necessary thing—which it is—it occurred to me that perhaps the aloneness He experienced might have been a bit lonely on occasion.

Take a look with me at John 8:1.

> *But Jesus went to the Mount of Olives.*

At first glance, there's nothing here to bring on wistfulness, right? However, when we read the verse in context, adding the verse that precedes it (John 7:53), we get the full picture:

> *And everyone went to his own house.*
> *But Jesus went to the Mount of Olives.*

Jesus left the town of Jerusalem and went to the hillside of the Mount of Olives to spend the night. This thought jars my soul. Those whom He taught during the day at the Temple went to their own homes at night, but Jesus made His way to the countryside to find shelter. It brings fresh meaning to His words, "Foxes have holes and birds of the air *have* nests, but the Son of Man has nowhere to lay *His* head" (Matthew 8:20).

What are your thoughts about the aloneness of Jesus? Do you think aloneness was a necessary part of his ministry and calling? Why or why not?

Now, to "the woman standing in the midst." I wonder what she was thinking. Did she know that Jesus was the only One in that crowd without sin? By His own directive, He was the only one qualified to cast that first stone. Perhaps if she did know this about Him, she also knew there was nobody who hated sin more than He did. And if she knew that, then maybe she knew there was none more compassionate toward sinners.

Yes, we know what's coming next, because we've read the Book. But holding this still frame in my heart right now, I'm just giddy with anticipation for her!

Today's Touchpoint

I hope your spiritual imagination got ramped up today as we continued to think about what Jesus wrote on the ground and what might have been going on in the hearts and minds of those who were present. You've seen the phrase "imagine with me," or something similar, a number of times throughout our study. I want to make sure you understand what I mean when I invite you to go exploring with me in this way.

First, facts are critical to Bible study. Studying the culture and context of a passage and reading what scholars say about it are essential if we are to understand and interpret the Bible appropriately. As followers of the One whose name is Truth, we must unwaveringly be committed to the truth, His Truth. So when I encourage you to imagine, I'm not leading you in the opposite direction of truth but encouraging you to develop your spiritual intellect.

We have a very creative God; just look at His world around us. I believe that the creativity God has given us, which we tap into with our imaginations, deserves special attention. Imagination helps us to visualize in our minds the things that our eyes cannot see. In fact, faith is the perfect picture of spiritual imagination, for it requires us to envision what we cannot perceive with our senses at the moment. If you can't imagine, how can you have faith?

Give your imagination a workout with the following exercise.

Travel back in time to spend a day with *Shame*—or one of the other biblical girlfriends we have met so far. Think about what you'd like to know, in addition to what you do know, about her and her story. Share your thoughts in writing below or in a journal. Enjoy, and have a great imaginary fieldtrip!

Dear Father, I'm growing to love the Bible more and more. Thank You for the word pictures You are placing in my heart as I study these anonymous women. I'm beginning to see You more clearly in my own life because I'm envisioning how You were at work in the lives of these women. Teach me how to appropriately use my creativity as I explore and study the Scriptures. I love You. Amen.

Day 4: The Look That Changes Your Life

Focus: Getting Cleaned Up in Jesus

Scripture:

[10]When Jesus had raised Himself up and saw no one but the woman, He said to her, "Woman, where are those accusers of yours? Has no one condemned you?" [11]She said, "No one, Lord." And Jesus said to her, "Neither do I condemn you; go and sin no more."

John 8:10-11

I received the following note from a woman who found freedom from shame in Jesus.

Through all my growing up years, my dad had a drinking problem. He would often become very angry and violent. As a result of the insecurity, fear, dread, and anxiety, I developed some dark habits. This caused me to feel deeply ashamed. I prayed for years that God would deliver me, promising Him over and over that I would stop damaging my body. My shame and guilt only grew. Then, through a relationship with Jesus Christ, I found grace and freedom from shame. He also freed me from the fear of what others thought about me. I'm so thankful He sees me through the perfection of His Son, Jesus. I am forgiven, beautiful, and accepted.

~ Anonymous

There's no cleansing like Jesus' cleansing! God placed human beings in a world that was perfect, but that world was soon defiled with sin when they chose their own way over God's way. Even before the filth of sin gave way to shame, God had devised a plan to cleanse humankind through His Son, Jesus. And before Jesus came to earth, God established rituals of sacrificial offerings for His people that foreshadowed the cleansing of Jesus to come—sacrifices that served as a temporary method of cleansing before the Lord. In fact, one could not be right with God apart from these sacrificial rituals. The Bible tells us that God hates sin and cannot look upon it (Habakkuk 1:13). These rituals were mandated by God to remind His people of their sinful condition, which made them unfit to draw near to a holy God, and of their need for a sacrificial atonement to be made right with God.

Imagine the life of an Israelite living during Old Testament times. In addition to sin, there were other things that could make one unclean. Numbers 5:2 lists a few examples:

Command the Israelites to send out from the camp anyone with a skin disease,
an oozing discharge, or who has become unclean by contact with a corpse. (CEB)

We devoted some study time to what it meant to be categorized as "unclean" during our exploration of the hemorrhaging woman in Mark 5. We also saw that anyone could become defiled by coming in contact with one who was unclean. Such an individual would then need to follow God's procedure for being declared clean.

Read Numbers 19. As someone who lives on this side of the cross, briefly describe your thoughts about this passage.

Now read Psalm 51. After considering the plea of David, write verse 12 below.

I've asked the Lord many times to "restore to me the joy of [His] salvation." As my love has increased for Him, so has my sensitivity to my sin nature. I'm more aware of the ways I mess up, and it saddens me when I do. I'm also very mindful of the reality of Romans 3:23, which reminds us, "All have sinned and fall short of the glory of God."

The Greek word for sin in Romans 3:23 is *hamartanō*, which means "to miss the mark" or "to wander from the path of uprightness."[3] This implies something different from deliberately choosing to sin. I long to be pure like God in thought and behavior, but the deeper I understand His nature, the more I become aware of my own. As human beings, we have a propensity to miss the mark or wander away from doing right.

In Psalm 51:3 we see a different word used to describe David's sin. It is the Hebrew word *pesha`*, which is translated "transgression" or "rebellion."[4] This conveys a deliberate choice to sin. So sin can be both intentional and unintentional. We all know this from personal experience, don't we? In either case, we are falling far short of God's goodness and glory.

How would you compare your sin nature to the holiness of God?

How does Isaiah 64:6 describe our contaminated status before the Lord?

Yes, in and of ourselves we are rotten to the core in comparison to God and His righteousness. I've heard those ignorant of this fact claim that goodness is enough to earn favor with God. The idea is that "if you're good enough, you're worthy enough." But the Bible doesn't back up that idea. Whether our sin is flat out rebellion or missing the mark of what's right, every single one of us is included in the "all" of Romans 3:23.

The blood of goats and bulls and the ashes of a heifer sprinkled on those who are ceremonially unclean sanctify them so that they are outwardly clean. How much more, then, will the blood of Christ, who through the eternal Spirit offered himself unblemished to God, cleanse our consciences from acts that lead to death, so that we may serve the living God! (Hebrews 9:13-14 NIV)

Take a look at Hebrews 9:13-14 (above). List the two methods of becoming clean before God described here: the old covenant procedure and the new covenant one.

Oh friend, aren't you thrilled to live during new covenant days? Until we go back and study those Old Testament rituals and procedures for approaching God, we have little appreciation for what the blood of Jesus Christ accomplished for us! We no longer have ashes of dead animals sprinkled on our bodies with hyssop by the High Priest to cleanse us. Instead, we enter God's presence through the grace of His Son, Jesus Christ, whose blood shed on the cross paid our sin debt and made a way for us to be reconciled to God. Hebrews 10:22 assures us that because of what Christ has done for us, we can draw near to God with confidence:

> *Let us draw near with a true heart in full assurance of faith, having our hearts sprinkled from an evil conscience and our bodies washed with pure water.*

● ● ● ● ● ●

Before continuing, take a few moments to thank God for His indescribable love gift, Jesus. Write your thoughts below.

Now we're ready to rejoin our girlfriend *Shame* as she encounters the love and grace of Jesus. Yesterday we captured a still frame in our hearts from John 8:9: "And Jesus was left alone, and the woman standing in the midst." Now, let your mind slowly move forward to Jesus rising from that kneeling position and coming face to face with *Shame*. Insert a holy drum-roll!

Don't rush through this image. Allow your heart to linger here and feel the gloriously beautiful moment when the eyes of Grace looked into the eyes of this sinful woman. Describe the moment here in your own words.

Being a romanticist at heart, it's honestly difficult for me to express my thoughts about what took place then. I love imagining it, thinking of it as a spiritual betrothal. How must she have felt going from ashamed and exposed to transparently pure? And it happened in an instant with His gaze! At least that's how I imagine it. We are not given the intimate details of what happened in that split second between them. I simply choose to believe it was a riveting moment—one that changed the rest of her life. What do *you* think?

Why do you think we often gloss over such details when reading God's Word?

Why it is important to enter into the story and meditate on these moments?

Jesus said, "Woman, where are those accusers of yours? Has no one condemned you?" (v. 10b). The Greek word used here for "accusers" is *katēgoros*, a name given to the devil by the rabbis.[5] It's the same word that is used in Revelation 12:10.

> *Then I heard a loud voice saying in heaven, "Now salvation, and strength, and the kingdom of our God, and the power of His Christ have come, for the accuser of our brethren, who accused them before our God day and night, has been cast down."*

This shouldn't surprise us, but it should enlighten us to the fact that ungodly conduct is prompted by the devil, the accuser.

After asking where her accusers were, Jesus asked, "Has no one condemned you?" Perhaps He spoke loudly enough for those who had slipped away to hear. In any case, it seems obvious that these words were spoken to give encouragement and boldness to her heart.

Jesus asked two questions, but the woman only answered one of them. Write below the question that she answered, followed by her response. (John 8:10-11)

It seems as though she is filled with respect for Jesus during these moments. She replies, "No one, Lord." Not only does she call Him Lord; but instead of focusing on His dealings with the ones who'd dragged her before Him, she focuses on what concerns *her*. This is a wonderful reminder for each of us to be more caught up in "Jesus and me" rather than being so concerned with "Jesus and them."

Next, a beautifully freeing thing happens. Jesus gives her His absolution: "Neither do I condemn you." This woman, who had been held captive by a sinful lifestyle that led to public degradation, was freed from shame and guilt in the forgiving heart of Jesus Christ.

Freed from shame. Take a moment to go back and reread the note written by the contemporary anonymous woman at the beginning of today's lesson. Both of these precious women, at the moment they were seen through the perfection of Jesus Christ, were forgiven and accepted.

There are many situations in life that can bring us shame. I have questions for you: Where are *your* accusers? Has anyone (or anything) condemned you? Perhaps there is something you'd like to erase from your past and your memory. Just the fleeting thought of it fills you with condemnation and sorrow. It's time for you to look deeply into the face and heart of your Savior and hear His powerfully gentle words, "Neither do I condemn you."

Let's explore some of the things that can "accuse" us and cause us to feel shame. Circle any that resonate with you personally:

thoughts	gossip	body language	looks (positive or negative)
whispers	disapproval	unforgiveness	low self-esteem
pride	expectations	self-confidence	education (too much/too little)
shame	humiliation	body image	popularity (too much/too little)
guilt	failure	disrespect	intellect (too much/too little)

other: _____

The enemy can use anything or anyone to fill the bill of an accuser.

Perhaps you are hearing the shouts of GUILTY, SHAMEFUL, or SINFUL to your spiritual ear right now. If so, then good for you! That's the first step. Think of it: those accusers who dragged this woman to Jesus actually did her a favor! Remember, sometimes the worst things can become the best things. It may be a bit tough, but can you by faith thank your heavenly Father for this avenue of getting you to Him? Remember, He does not cause sin, but He certainly will take a sinful situation and turn it around for His glory. I've seen it happen time and time again.

Can you recall an experience when God brought His glory out of sin? Make a few notes below.

Once again, review the exhilarating promise found in Romans 8:1 and write it below:

After Jesus forgave her, He commanded her, "Go and sin no more" (v. 11b). And that's where this remarkable storyline drops off—except in our imaginations. So what do you think? Was she so radically changed in that moment with Jesus that she made a new commitment to walk in His purity?

Jesus has forgiven you, too, and He commands you, "Go and sin no more." Are you so caught up in His love and forgiveness that you will commit to going and sinning no more?

You may wonder how it is possible to live sinless in a world full of sin. I haven't been able to get my brain wrapped around the answer to that question. I know that the Holy Spirit who lives inside us is our helper and promises to provide a way out of every sin (see John 14:26, Romans 8:2-6, and 1 Corinthians 10:13). Still, I've come to the conclusion that it isn't for me to reason it out but only to strive to do right and rely on the Holy Spirit within me. My heartfelt prayer is that those around me would see Christ in me and join me in loving Him and living for Him. Won't you join me in praying the same, girlfriend?

Today's Touchpoint

We shared a beautiful moment today, the moment when Jesus and the woman came face to face. One of the things I enjoy about getting into Scripture is that I see myself in the passages. As we close today, I want you to come alongside me in entering the story, replacing the details of this anonymous woman with the particulars of your own life. Picture yourself coming face to face with Jesus in a moment where you, fully aware of your sinful condition, encounter His amazing grace. Take your time, enjoying your spiritual betrothal. May our Father tremendously bless you as you seek deeper intimacy with Him.

If you like, make a few notes about the experience below or in a journal.

Dear heavenly Father, thank You so much for loving me in the deep way that You do. May I be even more deeply in love with You. Amen.

Day 5: The Spirit Behind the Law

Focus: My True Identity

Scripture:

Then Jesus spoke to them again, saying, "I am the light of the world. He who follows Me shall not walk in darkness, but have the light of life."

John 8:12

I will give you a new heart and put a new spirit within you; I will take the heart of stone out of your flesh and give you a heart of flesh.

Ezekiel 36:26

This week our emphasis has been on the woman who committed adultery, as highlighted in John 8. Personally, I think this passage is not as much about the sin of this woman as it is about her new identity in Jesus. A new life in Christ means that His Spirit lives within us. "In Him we live and move and have our being," according to the apostle Paul's words in Acts 17:28a. Yes, the adulterous woman was given new life and new opportunity to move within God's love. In our own lives, as well as in our assessments of the lives of others, may we be more eager to focus on new life in Christ rather than remain fixated on a particular sin.

Can you think of a personal example where you need to become preoccupied with new life in Christ instead of other issues? Explain.

In the conversation with the woman at the well, Jesus revealed Himself as the Living Water. Now, in another remarkable declaration, He lifts His gaze to those gathered there in the Temple courtyard and dramatically reveals Himself this time as the light of the world.

Perhaps He made this announcement just moments before the courtyard lamps were lit—a holy metaphor of God's Light overpowering the darkness of sin that had invaded the world. The lamps in the Temple courtyard provided light for celebration during the evening feasts. Even more so, Jesus becomes our Light, giving us opportunity to sing and celebrate in the midst of the darkness of this world.

Can you describe a moment when Jesus, your Light, caused you to celebrate during a dark moment?

Recall the conversation that Jesus had with the Samaritan woman in John 4:24. How did He tell her we must worship?

Now turn to Matthew 5:17. What statement did Jesus make concerning His role with the law?

Continue reading verses 18-31. In your own words, explain what you think Jesus meant when He said He came to fulfill the law.

As the fulfillment of the law, Jesus calls us to a higher standard than law-keeping. Worshiping in spirit and truth goes much deeper than simply agreeing to words spoken or written on paper. Perhaps the contracts I made during my days as a classroom teacher will illustrate my point. As I signed each contract, I pledged my heartfelt intention to be the best teacher I could be that year. That was signing in spirit, as opposed to merely agreeing to fulfill another year's tenure.

When Jesus says that He came to fulfill the law, He is referring to the deeper meaning of the law. He's talking about the spirit of the law, not merely the statement of it. As I reflected on this, I sensed the Lord speaking these words to my spirit: "Don't let the law blind you to the real meaning behind it." It's easy to adhere to what's on paper, but there's so much more! Oh my, we are so inclined to look merely at the surface instead of exploring the depths, aren't we? I'm learning and loving the process of going deeper and deeper with Him. I'm praying this is also becoming reality for you, my friend.

Can you think of a time when the "letter of the law" blinded you to the spirit behind it? If so, briefly describe it below.

Since the seventh commandment, "You shall not commit adultery" (Exodus 20:14), has been at the center of our story this week, let's take a look at the spirit behind this law for us as Christians. We know adultery to be the violation of the marriage contract through intimacy with a partner outside of that marriage. Usually we define this as a physical act. However, if we are to uphold the spirit behind the law, then we must also include emotional intimacy outside of the marriage as adultery. Oh my friend, if we don't explore the emotional realm of adultery, we are missing a huge part of God's intention in this commandment. Emotional adultery can cause just as much damage in a marriage as can physical adultery.

Pause and talk with your heavenly Father about these two areas of adultery (physical and emotional). You may write your thoughts below or keep them between you and Jesus, but spend a few moments here.

There's one more type of adultery for us to examine. It's called *spiritual adultery*. Yesterday, we briefly explored the idea of being spiritually betrothed to the Lord. The Scriptures are replete with Christ being depicted as the Bridegroom and the church as His Bride. If we are genuine followers of Jesus, then we are indeed *married* to Christ. He alone can meet our every need. In turn, we are to seek only Him to ultimately fulfill those needs. The moment we turn to other people and other things to become the fulfiller of those needs, we commit spiritual adultery.

This is not to say that we cannot have expectations for those we love. My point here is that no other human can possibly meet the many needs we have. God designed it that way so that we would become dependent upon Him as our Provider and the One who meets every desire of our hearts.

The most freeing gift I ever gave my husband was releasing him from the responsibility of meeting all of my needs. I'm blessed that he loves me with a passion, but I'm even more blessed to realize my Lord as the ultimate Lover of my life. I'm a very emotionally needy person, so this decision was also the greatest gift I gave to myself in our marriage.

From personal experience I can vouch for the truth that the best thing for marriage is to love God first and your spouse second. This is why God commands it. You'll find the basis for this guideline in Deuteronomy 6:5, which later is echoed by Jesus in Matthew 22:37-39.

Jesus said to him, "'You shall love the Lord your God with all your heart, with all your soul, and with all your mind.' This is the first and great commandment. And the second is like it: 'You shall love your neighbor as yourself.'" (Matthew 22:37-39)

Read Matthew 22:37-39 above. Give an example of how to apply this instruction to marriage.

Explain in your own words how depending upon another to satisfy your soul can be classified as *spiritual adultery*.

It's easy to see this concept played out in the lives of the Israelites in the Old Testament. They habitually transgressed against God by "hooking up" with the heathen nations around them. They took on their customs, along with their gods. They knew better! So do we, my friend. Spiritual adultery was not only a problem in the Old Testament; it's ongoing today between God and those who love Him.

Looking back at my own life, I see that I've been guilty of this very thing. Here are some personal transgressions that come to mind:

Expecting my husband to meet all of my needs
Finding my self-esteem in what others think of me
Enjoying times with others more than I enjoy time with the Lord
Not spending adequate time to grow in intimacy with God

I could give many other examples from the pages of my life's story. What about you?

Where is there spiritual adultery in your life? What are some of the ways you have placed other people and things before the Lord?

Roughly two thousand years ago, our sister who was dragged before Jesus wound up being dipped into the cleansing waters of forgiveness. With His light flooding her mind and heart, grace washed over and through her. The freedom she experienced in letting go of those lesser lovers is the same freedom that could be yours right at this very moment.

Spend some quiet moments with Jesus talking about the lesser lovers in your life. Ask Him to help you let go of them and place Him first. If you like, write your thoughts or a prayer below.

In Ezekiel 36:26 we find this promise:

> *I will give you a new heart and put a new spirit within you; I will take the heart of stone out of your flesh and give you a heart of flesh.*

Stone in this verse is used metaphorically to describe hardness. Whether this hardness is an indifference or harshness of attitude, God has a replacement that's far better! His new heart is one renewed by the Spirit via God's grace.

I believe that our friend in the temple courtyard experienced the removal of her stony heart by the hands of the skilled Surgeon Himself—as He gazed deeply into her soul. I imagine Him performing the holy procedure of replacing that dulled-by-sin heart of hers with a living and vibrant new one; and as He removed the old heart, He filled her new heart with His affections and desires, enveloped by fresh delight.

Though we're not told this in the text, we know the wonder-working marvels of God's grace that He freely lavishes upon His children (see 2 Corinthians 5:17 and 1 Peter 2:21).

My friend, you can keep your heart fresh in Him by remembering that your identity is found in Jesus alone. You can choose to saturate your mind with life-changing Scriptures that will serve as ongoing reminders of His unconditional love for you. You can choose to trust Him to meet every desire of your heart instead of turning to incapable lovers. If you have made the all-important decision to turn your life over to Jesus Christ, your identity is locked in the heart of Christ!

Today's Touchpoint

We're ending an awesome week of study. As I've moved through the writing of this content, my prayer has been that our gracious Father would show you how to be released from shame and any residue it has left upon your heart. There's simply no place for it, my friend. Jesus and shame cannot reside together.

You may be thinking, *Wait, I am a Christian, but I still struggle with shame from my past; how can that be?* Shame is a tactic of the enemy of our souls (remember, the Bible says that he is the accuser). Negative thoughts or emotions that are condemning or based in fear are not from God, such as anxiety, worry, false guilt, doubts, and so forth. Certainly the thoughts and feelings are real, but they are not placed there by God. Remember, once you acknowledge and confess your sins to God, the issue is settled.

Long ago, I memorized 1 John 1:9, and I quote it anytime I need the reminder.

If we confess our sins, He is faithful and just to forgive us our sins and to cleanse us from all unrighteousness. (1 John 1:9)

Write 1 John 1:9 on a card or slip of paper or a note in your phone or tablet. Keep it with you and tuck it inside your heart and mind.

Years ago, God gave me a powerful tool to deal with those foreign thoughts that try to slip in and invade my peace of mind. One day while writing away on another book, I answered a phone call. Something in the conversation triggered an unpleasant memory that I'd already dealt with and put away. After the conversation was over, it was difficult getting my mind back on track. God's audible, inaudible voice spoke to my spirit: "You do not have to take this, and you can do something about it!"

Next, the Holy Spirit called to mind Matthew 4, the passage where Jesus is being tempted by Satan at the end of His forty-day fast in the wilderness. The holy zoom-in was on Matthew 4:10 (NIV): "Away from me, Satan! For it is written: 'Worship the Lord your God, and serve him only.'"

As I recalled the verse, God said to my spirit, "You can pray the words of Jesus and be victorious!" He simply revealed to me that any time I was hit with a thought that I knew was from the enemy, I could pray, "Get out of here, Satan, I'm worshiping the Lord my God, and He only am I serving!" Then, the Holy Spirit gunned His holy engine within me with this thought: "If you allow those ungodly thoughts to take you captive by consuming your thoughts and emotions, it's as though you are no longer worshiping Me."

Right then God birthed in me a sacred strategy for dealing with the fiery darts of the enemy. He also gave me a visual. Later that day, a little black o-ring appeared in a box I was rummaging through. I immediately picked it up and placed it on my finger, dubbing it my Matthew 4:10 ring. I wore this little black ring for years until I learned to automatically kick the enemy out without seeing the visual reminder. During the years that have followed, it has been such a sweet pleasure to share this concept with others. We must be proactive in encouraging each other with the encouragement we receive from the Lord. So, here's your review:

1. The enemy hurls a fiery dart your way.
2. Turn it on him by saying, "Get outta here, Satan, I'm worshiping the Lord my God; He alone do I serve!"

As we close this week's study, I'm commissioning you to secure a Matthew 4:10 visual reminder. It may be a ring, a necklace, a bracelet, or some other reminder. And remember; you are not by yourself. You have Christ on the inside of you, as well as others who love Him and love you surrounding you and spurring you on.

O Father, how can I adequately say "Thanks" for all the things You have done for me? The truths You place in my heart are exactly what I need to live a life of victory in You. Show me how to walk in Your grace and how to help others do the same. How I love You! Amen.

Video Viewer Guide

If we confess our sins, He is faithful and just to forgive us our sins and to cleanse us from all unrighteousness.

1 John 1:9 NKJV

We are not only free from the _____;

we are free from the _____ of it.

A lesson from Jesus' encounter with the religious leaders:

God always gives us the _____.

A lesson from Jesus' encounter with the woman:

[Jesus] does not throw stones at us when we _____ _____.

Therefore, if anyone is in Christ, [she] is a _____

_____; old things have passed away; behold, all things

have become new.

2 Corinthians 5:17 NKJV

Week 6
Rhythm of Grace
New Name, New Identity

Our Story and Memory Verse

28-30 "Are you tired? Worn out? Burned out on religion? Come to me. Get away with me and you'll recover your life. I'll show you how to take a real rest. Walk with me and work with me—watch how I do it. Learn the unforced rhythms of grace. I won't lay anything heavy or ill-fitting on you. Keep company with me and you'll learn to live freely and lightly."

Matthew 11:28-30 *The Message*

Our New Name: The Promise of What's to Come

I love this passage. Just reading it calms me and brings me back to my spiritual roots. It's all about walking in sweet rhythm with the Lover of my soul—a fitting Scriptural theme for our concluding week. Throughout our study we have been considering what it means to draw closer to Jesus and discover our identity in the very heart of God. And as we do, we learn the rhythm of grace.

Thinking back, I realize this holy cadence has varied throughout the phases of my life, but it has always been there. I want to encourage and challenge you. Whatever your chapter of life at the moment, quiet yourself enough to hear God's holy rhythm. Keeping time with His tempo will help you maintain a steady and relaxed lifestyle. This week, we'll explore simple yet glorious truths to aid your spiritual ears in hearing the beat of His heart as He draws you more deeply into His love.

Memorize Matthew 11:28-30 from *The Message* Bible (see preceding page) as you make your way through this final week. Write below your own plan or strategy for committing this verse to memory.

Getting to the last week of a Bible study has always been difficult for me. As a participant in studies during the early years of my Christian walk, it was sad to think about the relationship I'd shared with the author and other ladies in our study group coming to an end. Through the journey, I'd particularly enjoyed and depended upon the writer's spiritual insights into God's Word. Even her *spiritual conjectures* about the unknowns seemed to be more credible than anything I would have dared to imagine. These respected and notable Bible teachers were quick to affirm that others could enjoy the same relationship with Jesus by simply applying themselves to God's Word and seeking His heart. I would always dismiss that comment as one made in humility and deference to God's love for each of His children. In the inner longings of my heart, I could not imagine going deeper with the Lord until I embarked on the next Bible study, which I believed would provide the holy parameters needed for me to grow in my journey.

How thankful I am that our God in His bigness embraced me in my smallness, including *me* in His great heart of love! Many years before He called the likes of me to write a Bible study, He called me to a love relationship that was all inclusive. I did not have to depend upon those more scholarly than I to teach me how to grow in love with Him. My dear sister, hear His call. While I have prayed all along that the material in this Bible study would draw you deeply into relationship with Him, know that it's never God's intent that you rely on *another's* walk or spiritual insights to determine the depth of your relationship with Him.

Consider the past six weeks as a fresh jumpstart to your love life with Jesus. It's true that through the years of my ministry of speaking and writing, I've grown so much in my knowledge of the Lord. I've also come to a depth in my relationship with Him that is far beyond anything I'd ever imagined. But the reason is no mystery, nor is it reserved for those who write Bible studies or speak from the platform. It is the result of a love life with Jesus nurtured with time and desire. Through the years my desire to know Him has deepened. Like you, I've traveled through phases where the demands of life kept me from spending as much time with Him as I wanted. But, my friend, God is faithful. He hears your heart, and when you come to Him with love and desire, He will satisfy your longing to know Him in a deeper and more intimate way. Just keep placing your request before Him, and listen to the Holy Spirit's response as He helps you creatively determine how to spend time with Him.

Even in this chapter of my life as an author, it's still difficult to come to the final week of a study. I feel a responsibility to have a grand finale of sorts—you know, one that will leave you with holy zings of insight and electrified emotions. But this morning as I sought God's heart in worship, He brought me back to His simplicity and unforced rhythm of grace. In my musings with Him, He brought to mind the reality of what He wants with each of His children: to enjoy Him by simply being you—that special somebody you are. He has given you a personality, a calling, and gifts to equip you to live life to the fullest within His unforced rhythm of grace. And as we'll see this week, we have much to look forward to—both in this life and in the life to come.

Just as our four anonymous girlfriends met Jesus and were forever changed, so we are changed by drawing close to Him. Not only do we receive a new identity, but one day we also will receive a new name! It's the promise of what's to come.

Let's begin this final week of our study by returning our focus to our four friends. Each of them stepped out of the pages of Scripture after her encounter with Jesus, but I have no doubt that each was deeply humbled by His love and challenged to live life from this new perspective. Like our biblical girlfriends, as we step out of this study may we embrace a fresh and holy challenge to live life deeply humbled by the love of our Lord. And as we keep company with Him, may we learn to live freely and lightly, knowing that we are forever changed by His grace.

Day 1: New Name

Focus: Getting Excited About What's to Come

Scripture:

Anyone who has an ear should listen to what the Spirit says to the churches. I will give the victor some of the hidden manna. I will also give him a white stone, and on the stone a new name is inscribed that no one knows except the one who receives it.

Revelation 2:17 HCSB

All of our grandbabies have had makeshift names for their life-in-the-womb days. We talked about them and addressed them by their pseudonyms during the entire nine months before their natural births. Little Bug, Sweet Pea, Peanut, Toodles, Woodchip, and ButterBiscuit—each found a special niche in this Gigi's heart. Little identities attached themselves to these whimsical names, giving me a special bond with these babies even before they ventured onto planet Earth. These names were just holding names until they received their real given names by their parents.

You, my friend, have a holding-name, too. It's the name you're known by during your days on earth—your given name. A given name is "the name given to one, as distinguished from an inherited family name."[1]

You also have an inherited family name—the last name that you share with other members of your family. However, if you have turned control of your life over to Jesus as your Lord, then you also are a member of God's family and have another inherited family name: *Christian*.

As God's child, you have something to look forward to, my friend. When you come face to face with the Lord, you will receive a brand new name. According to Revelation 2:17, each of His children will be given a new name by King Jesus Himself. And here's the fun part: this name is so intimate that it will be a secret between you and Him. Isn't that the coolest thing ever!

Let me pause and say that if you happen to find yourself in a fuddy-duddy and stodgy relationship with Jesus—one that has lost its excitement—let this verse from the Book of Revelation snap you right out of it! Our God is the Master of creativity, mystery, and excitement. Let your mind become engaged with holy wonder about the things to come. Imagine, dream, and celebrate the newness and freshness of your Lord.

Stop now and imagine what name the Lord might give to you on a white stone. You have no way of knowing what it will be, so just enjoy imagining. Share your thoughts in the space provided on the next page or in your journal.

Wasn't that fun? Of all the things you've learned through this study, I surely hope one of them is how to have fun with the Lord! Now it's time to dig into this curious verse and enjoy what God's Word reveals.

The book of Revelation was written when the church was in its beginning years. John was caught up in a revelation from God and was told to write what he saw. Revelation 2:17 was part of a message addressed to one of the seven churches in Asia at the time John wrote these messages. The future seemed unsure and many believers were afraid of being strong enough to stand up to the adversities they would face. Jesus wanted these believers to know that He understood exactly how they felt and what they were going through. He wanted them to know that He reigned as Mighty Conqueror in their midst and that through Him they could overcome.

These messages are for believers in our day as well—not only for the church collectively but also for each of us individually. In the book of Revelation, Jesus gives us His end time plan. He also pronounces a blessing on all who read, hear, and keep those things that are written in this prophecy (see Revelation 1:3).

We'll talk about the hidden manna mentioned in Revelation 2:17 later this week. Today our focus is the white stone on which is written the new name that will be given to each of us by Jesus. Since Revelation 2:17 is the only reference in the Bible to it, it's all the more mysterious. Here is one of several common interpretations that makes sense to me.

In ancient Greece, jury members would cast a white stone to signify an acquittal, whereas a black stone proclaimed the defendant guilty.[2] Christ's sacrifice on the cross pronounces us innocent when we are indeed guilty. What a joy it will be to receive this white stone of remembrance as a gift from the One who has delivered us and set us free. That we will be able to hold it in the hand of our glorified body is a thrilling thought!

The Greek word for this stone, *psephos*, describes it as being one that is worn smooth or polished.[3] And *leukos*, the Greek word for white, means brilliantly white, as in garments of angels.[4] It will be some gem, right?

Personally, I like to think that this stone has been worn and polished by the trials of life. Think with me about the prophet Isaiah's words.

Read Isaiah 40:1-5 and answer the following questions.

What does God say He will do to every valley?

Every mountain?

The crooked places?

The rough places?

All of us have some valleys, mountains, and crooked and rough places in our lives. For me, every time I've become submissive to God and have depended upon Him to bring me through such trials, it seems He has smoothed me out through the process. *As life wears me down, God has a way of lifting me up!*

Take a few moments to think about that concept, and then briefly share an experience of your own.

An experience of life wearing me down and God lifting me up:

I don't know if we'll be thinking of these particulars when Jesus gives us our white stone. Probably not. But I do believe we'll be completely aware of the fact that it was through Him that we were victorious overcomers in all of life's trials.

Let's come full circle as we close today. What about the name on that stone? Being the romantic that I am, I totally believe this new name will be one that will have sweet significance between my Lord and me. It may have to do with a certain struggle I endured through His grace. Or maybe it will signify a change in my heart birthed through trusting Him by faith. Whatever my new name will be, it will be sweetly appropriate for me, just as yours will be for you. I just love dreaming about this moment—how about you?

Today's Touchpoint

I hope that today's lesson has been spiritually invigorating for you and that your heart has beat with celebration for what's to come between you and the Lord. Let's wind up by stretching your imagination just a bit further.

Reflecting on what we've studied today and the names we've given in this study to our anonymous women from Scripture, what *new name* would you give to each woman? Rename each woman with a name that you feel signifies her new identity after her encounter with Jesus.

New name for *Judged*: _____

New name for *Hurting*: _____

New name for *Ordinary*: _____

New name for *Shame*: _____

Dear heavenly Father, thank You for teaching and leading me to explore Your creative love for me. What a mysterious and joy-filled promise we find in Revelation 2:17! Keep me looking forward to all the wonderfully breathtaking new things You have in store for me. Forgive me when I get bored or complacent in our relationship. Help me to stay fresh and excited about the love that we share. Amen.

Day 2: Victory Stones

Focus: Celebrating God's Faithfulness

Scripture:

*Then Samuel took a stone and set it up between Mizpah and Shen, and called its name Ebenezer, saying, "Thus far the L*ORD *has helped us."*

1 Samuel 7:12

This verse about the Ebenezer stone, which we will explore today, made a dramatic impact upon my life many years ago, calling me to a new place of determined celebration for all that God has done for me. As God's children, it's very important that celebration be ongoing in our lives. Dismissing and forgetting to celebrate God's goodness is taking for granted all the wonderful things He does for us. Collecting stones can be a practical way to help us remember to celebrate.

One of my favorite works of Christian fiction is the allegorical novel by Hannah Hurnard, *Hinds' Feet on High Places*, which takes its title from Habakkuk 3:19: "The LORD God is my strength, and he will make my feet like hinds' feet, and he will make me to walk upon mine high places" (KJV). The story is about an insecure and deformed shepherdess who longs to journey to the high places with the Good Shepherd. Like *Judged, Hurting, Ordinary*, and *Shame*, she has a name that represents her character: *Much Afraid*. As *Much Afraid* encounters the daunting obstacles that line her path to the high places, she gathers stones and places them in a little bag, which she carries next to her heart. Each stone is a reminder of the Good Shepherd's love and promise to her. His promise is that she will make it to the high places if she trusts Him to take her there. The stones she collects as she overcomes each hardship serve as her visual reminders of the Good Shepherd's faithfulness to carry her through. They are reminders of His help during the difficulties that assault her along the way.

Why is it important to remind ourselves of those times of God's help in our lives?

Let's take a look now at the Ebenezer stone of 1 Samuel 7:12. *Ebenezer* is defined as "stone of help."[5] It was set up by Samuel after a significant defeat of the Philistine army. The stone marked the spot where God had fought for the children of Israel that day. The Ebenezer was a memorial of God's help.

Let's consider the events that prompted Samuel to set aside this memorial stone.

> *Now as Samuel was offering up the burnt offering, the Philistines drew near to battle against Israel. But the LORD thundered with a loud thunder upon the Philistines that day, and so confused them that they were overcome before Israel. And the men of Israel went out of Mizpah and pursued the Philistines, and drove them back as far as below Beth Car. Then Samuel took a stone and set it up between Mizpah and Shen, and called its name Ebenezer, saying, "Thus far the LORD has helped us."*
>
> 1 Samuel 7:10-12

Samuel had been forthright with the Israelites, telling them they needed to put away their foreign gods and get back to serving the one true God. He went on to assure them that if they returned wholeheartedly, then God would deliver them from the hand of the Philistines. So the children of Israel put away their gods and gathered at the very place that previously they had experienced defeat. How appropriate for them to return to the field between Mizpah and Shen where their defeat had taken place. Because sin had captured their hearts and they had turned away from God, He had allowed the Philistines to capture them. This time, however, they came armed not with weapons but with prayer. Their purpose for gathering was to repent of their sins and turn back to God. This was a place of a renewed covenant and their renewed commitment.

When the Philistines realized the Israelites had gathered, they suspected there was a strategy of revolt materializing, so they made plans to once again go into battle with them. With war being imminent, the children of Israel pleaded with Samuel to cry out on their behalf. Samuel did, and God graciously answered his prayer. Confusion permeated the camp of the Philistines at the onset of battle, which caused them to succumb to defeat. God was mighty, swift, and victorious!

I love a good story of victory, especially a true Bible story! I've read this passage often, and each time I get caught up in Israel's victory over the Philistines. Do you know why? Because celebrating God's help and victory in this battle reminds me to celebrate His help and victory in my own.

Do you have some God-fought battles you need to actively celebrate? My friend, if our worship of God stays confined to the pages of His Word, we miss God's great purpose for celebration within our day-to-day living.

Let's celebrate! I'll help you get started by giving you a few biblical examples of God's help, then you can respond with your own.

1. God made a way for the Israelites to cross to dry land by parting the sea (Exodus 14:26-29). How has God made a way for you during a trial of life?

2. God commanded Joshua to be strong and courageous (Joshua 1:1-10). When has God filled you with His courage in a troubling situation?

3. The prophet Isaiah spoke to the Israelites with God's promise that they would run and not be weary, walk and not faint (Isaiah 40:31). When has God provided strength in a time of weariness?

4. When the disciples were filled with fear, Jesus calmed the storm (Matthew 8:23-27). Has the Lord ever filled you with His calmness when you were facing a fearful situation?

Dear friend, pause right now and thank God for His help in your life. Think of the examples you just listed, along with others that come to mind. Spend some moments in thanksgiving to Him. Record your thankfulness below or in your journal.

Here's one final take-away from our Bible passage for today. How sweet and powerful it is to return to a place of previous defeat and give God glory in a new situation. Just like the children of Israel, you can revisit a field of defeat and allow God to turn it into a field of victory through prayer and renewed commitment to the One Who is able to do all things!

Is God prompting you to take some action so that He can turn a previous field of defeat into a field of victory? Write your thoughts below.

As I think about reminders of turning defeat into victory, I can't help but consider *Judged*, *Hurting*, *Ordinary*, and *Shame*. Can you imagine your victorious reference point as the moment you encountered Jesus? And one day, friend, we will have the ultimate victory when we look into the face of Jesus. What a glorious moment yet ahead for us!

Today's Touchpoint

I hope you'll continue to think about the stone with your new name written on it that you and Jesus will share. That's my number one victory stone. But I have other victory stones that cause me to celebrate.

Years ago, influenced by the little shepherdess *Much Afraid* and Samuel the prophet, I began my own collection of Ebenezer stones. As I looked back at my life, I collected stones to represent God's help and victory in past trials. Soon God gave me fresh events for my stone ensemble. There were times when the Ebenezer wasn't a stone at all but some other item that represented God's faithfulness, such as a small piece of an X-ray that I kept after God healed our son from a tragic accident. You see, it doesn't matter what method you use to remember—only that you *do* remember.

So, can you guess how we're going to close this day? Today—or sometime this week—I encourage you to become a woman on a mission to find a pretty little bag and some gorgeous little stones to represent God's help and victory in past trials. Be creative and enjoy the ways God speaks to you as you determine to honor Him with your victory stones of remembrance!

Dear Father, forgive me for not thanking You often enough for the many times You've rescued me in this life. Right now I'm making a renewed commitment to live in continual praise and thanksgiving for all You do for me. With each stone of remembrance I collect, I will worship You with freshness of heart. I love You. Amen.

Day 3: The Name Above All Names

Focus: Calling on the Name of Jesus

Scripture:

"I am the Alpha and the Omega, the *Beginning and* the *End," says the Lord, "who is and who was and who is to come, the Almighty."*

Revelation 1:8

Today is a day of Scripture meditation, prayer, and journaling. My friend, if you are rushing to complete today's lesson, stop right now. Place this study aside, and come back to it later. The Holy Spirit has impressed upon my heart the importance of giving Him the honor and glory due His name as we study today. Together let's bring to Him our time as well as our hearts as we consider the Name above all names. It is with deep humility and reverence that I place us before the King of kings and Lord of lords in prayer:

Dear heavenly Father, right now my heart is filled with speechless wonder. It overwhelms me beyond words to know that You invite us to come before Your throne. It simply blows me away that You want to share Your glory with us. Here we are, Lord, Your fragile, unworthy girls stepping Your way. Thank You for bringing us into Your unconditional love as we approach. We love You. Amen.

Record the names given to Jesus in the following verses:

Revelation 1:17

Revelation 2:8

Revelation 22:13

He Who was in the very beginning and will be forever more knows how to rescue us from *all* of our stress and distress. And furthermore, He wants to! I've had the blessed opportunity to walk with the Lord for many years now, and I'm discovering that when the stresses of life cave in on me, my earthly world levels out if I can manage to direct my focus to Jesus as the Alpha and the Omega, the First and the Last, the Beginning and the End. In light of the magnitude of Who Jesus is—the all-encompassing nature of His power and His reign—everything else falls into proper perspective.

Take a few moments to prayerfully meditate on Jesus as the Alpha and Omega, the First and the Last, the Beginning and the End. How can you direct your focus to *this* picture of Jesus in a current situation in your life?

How does doing so change your perspective?

We've given much attention to names throughout our study, from the names we've given our four anonymous girlfriends—*Judged, Hurting, Ordinary,* and *Shame*—to our new names that will be written on brilliant and dazzling white stones. And today we are examining the name above all names, His Name:

> *Therefore God also has highly exalted Him and given Him the name which is above every name, that at the name of Jesus every knee should bow, of those in heaven, and of those on earth, and of those under the earth, and that every tongue should confess that Jesus Christ is Lord, to the glory of God the Father.*
> Philippians 2:9-11

Reread this verse aloud slowly. As you read, imagine what will take place in this holy moment. Write about what you visualize in the space below or in a journal.

When you come to know God in a way that brings rejoicing into your heart and life, you simply cannot wait for that awesome moment to bow down before Him! My heart is greatly grieved when I think of those who deny and dismiss the fact that one day they too will bow and confess Him as Lord.

Do you know someone who is not living in the excitement of bowing before Jesus as Lord? If so, pause now and pray for this person. Take several minutes to express your deep desire for this individual to know and reverence Jesus Christ as the Name above all names. Write a few words, phrases, or sentences below to summarize your heartfelt prayer.

"I am the Alpha and the Omega, the Beginning and the End." These are the words of Christ Himself. He is both the old covenant and the new covenant. He is both truth and grace. He is both the message and the fulfillment of the Scriptures. He is the One Who was, is, and is to come. He is responsible for our justification, our sanctification, and our glorification. He is our all in all.

How He *longs* to have relationship with those He created. Just think of Him announcing, "I am the Alpha and the Omega, the Beginning and the End." Through Jesus, God sought to make Himself known by coming to earth, sharing our lives, and speaking in ways we can understand. Although Christ is our beginning and our end, in reality He Himself knows no beginning or end. He is from eternity to eternity, from everlasting to everlasting. Yet from the beginning He wanted those He created to know Him. He chose not to be anonymous but to disclose His name!

To share a name is to make yourself known to others. God revealed His identity through His name. At the burning bush, God revealed a specific name to Moses.

> *Then Moses said to God, "Indeed, when I come to the children of Israel and say to them, 'The God of your fathers has sent me to you,' and they say to me, 'What is His name?' what shall I say to them?"*
>
> *And God said to Moses, "I Am Who I Am." And He said, "Thus you shall say to the children of Israel, 'I Am has sent me to you.'"*
>
> Exodus 3:13-14

It's kind of a mysterious name, wouldn't you agree? But as we've seen, God is all about mystery. At the same time, He's all about making Himself known to us in terms we can understand. He wants us to know Him, and He wants us to *want* to know Him. Yes, God is both mysterious and relational. In revealing His name as I Am, God makes the point that He is the God who is always present and always able.

How has God been present and able in your life?

Jesus—who was God in human flesh—also revealed Himself as I Am. On seven occasions in the Gospel of John, Jesus used an "I am" statement to describe Himself.

Read each Scripture and complete the statement of Jesus.

John 6:35 "I am_____."

John 8:12 "I am_____."

John 10:7 "I am_____."

John 10:11 "I am_____."

John 11:25 "I am_____."

John 14:6 "I am_____."

John 15:1 "I am_____."

How do these statements help us to understand Jesus' divinity?

Now read John 8:56-58 and 10:30-33. What was the people's response to Jesus when He revealed His identity on these two occasions?

In both instances Jesus equated Himself with God. In the first, He identified Himself as I Am, and in the second He said that He and the Father were one. Both times the people's violent response showed they clearly understood that Jesus was declaring Himself to be the eternal, incarnate God. How tragic it was that the incarnate God was physically in their midst yet they totally dismissed Him.

Are we dismissing Jesus today? Oh, not in the way of the people in His day who denied He was God. But do we sometimes disregard Him as the Alpha and Omega, the Beginning and End, the Name above all names in our lives? How tragic it is when we forget Who He is. May the reality of Who He is keep us humble and thankful every single moment of every day!

Today's Touchpoint

Do *you*, my sister, need an ever-present God who will rescue you and meet every one of your needs? You have One in the great I Am! He is the Name above all names!

Is God speaking to your heart with fresh revelation about Who He is and Who He wants to be in your life? Record your thoughts below or in a journal.

Reflect again on the needs that God met through Jesus in the lives of our four anonymous girlfriends, and describe them below:

Judged

Hurting

Ordinary

Shame

Dear heavenly Father, You are the great I Am. You are worthy to receive all glory and honor and power. I praise You. I honor You. I bow before You. Thank You, Father, for coming to earth as Jesus so that we could better understand Who You are and what You are like. Help me to realize and to remember that just as You met the needs of the biblical women we have been studying, so You meet my every need. You are my fulfillment, my all in all. Thank You. Amen.

Day 4: Hidden Manna

Focus: Being Nurtured by Jesus

Scripture:

Anyone who has an ear should listen to what the Spirit says to the churches. I will give the victor some of the hidden manna. I will also give him a white stone, and on the stone a new name is inscribed that no one knows except the one who receives it.

Revelation 2:17 HCSB

In the same verse where Jesus declares to give each of us a white stone with a new name written on it, He also states that overcomers will receive some of the hidden manna. Just as we don't fully understand the meaning of the white stone with our new name, so it's challenging to get our minds wrapped around the essence of the hidden manna. Ah, the mystery of God! Yet Bible study can be exhilarating if we don't get caught up in needing to have all of the answers and invite the Spirit to help us as we go digging for clues. The digging part is the fun part for me, because any insight into God's Word is life-changing and bolstering to my spirit. So, let's have some fun and dig!

First, let's take a look at the manna that God provided for the Israelites as they wandered around for forty years in the desert. They ate this food for *forty years*. That's some straight-up superfood right there!

We are introduced to this heavenly superfood in Exodus 16:

> *Then the Lord said to Moses, "Behold, I will rain bread from heaven for you. And the people shall go out and gather a certain quota every day, that I may test them, whether they will walk in My law or not."*

Exodus 16:4

Now read Exodus 16:31 and answer the following questions.

What did the Israelites call this bread from heaven?

What did it look like?

What did it taste like?

In Psalm 78, we read this beautiful description of the wilderness manna:

Yet He had commanded the clouds above,
And opened the doors of heaven,
Had rained down manna on them to eat,
And given them of the bread of heaven.
Men ate angels' food;
He sent them food to the full.
                                        Psalm 78:23-25

Oh my! What would it be like to eat the food that angels eat? The manna mystery continues.

Read Hebrews 9:4. What three things were placed in the ark of the covenant?

The manna was placed in the ark as a reminder of God's provision and faithfulness to the Israelites.

Now turn to 1 Kings 8:9. When the ark was opened, what was inside?

Somewhere between Moses placing the three items in the ark and Solomon having the ark brought to the Temple, the manna and Aaron's rod both disappeared. Although this disappearance remains a mystery, Jesus gave us some clues about the deeper symbolism of the manna and its connection to the Messiah:

I am the bread of life. Your fathers ate the manna in the wilderness, and they died. This is the bread that comes down from heaven so that anyone may eat of it and not die.

John 6:48-50 HCSB

What was the point that Jesus was making in this verse to the Jews who were listening to Him?

When we continue reading the next verse, we gain even more insight:

"I am the living bread that came down from heaven. Whoever eats this bread will live forever, and the bread that I will give for the life of the world is my flesh."

John 6:51 CEB

Jesus wanted to help them understand that He was the fulfillment of the old covenant. Whereas the manna of the old covenant was the bread of heaven provided for the Israelites in the wilderness, the manna of the new covenant was Jesus Himself—the living bread that came down from heaven.

Given what we've learned so far, why do you think Jesus refers to the manna as *hidden manna* in Revelation 2:17?

Biblical commentaries have much to say about this *hidden* manna. I like to think of it representing that which Christ has reserved for me—if I really want it. A Scripture from the prophet Jeremiah comes to mind: "You will seek Me and find *Me*, when you search for Me with all your heart" (Jeremiah 29:13). To me, flowing in the rhythm of the grace of Jesus is about searching for Him with a whole heart—and then receiving His revelations as a result. Jesus, our Hidden Manna, is ready to reveal to us as much as we want to know about Him. That knowledge, according to God's Word, is available when we seek it with our whole heart. As we seek Him and receive the fresh word of His manna, we are equipped to be overcomers through Jesus Christ.

But thanks be to God, who gives us the victory through our Lord Jesus Christ.

1 Corinthians 15:57

196   *Anonymous*

How are Jesus, manna, and overcomer all related?

According to 1 John 5:4-5, who is the overcomer (conqueror, victor)?

What could be spiritually "heftier" (carrying more spiritual weight or power) than to be an overcomer? I cannot think of this word without remembering Jesus' words in John 16:33:

> *"These things I have spoken to you, that in Me you may have peace. In the world you will have tribulation; but be of good cheer, I have **overcome** the world."* (emphasis added)

Yes, my friend, we are overcomers if Jesus Christ lives in our hearts. We may not always behave as overcomers, but that is what we are. Why? Because He lives inside us, and He is the One Who overcomes!

Why is it, then, that we don't always *feel* like conquerors? If that's often true of you, don't beat yourself up about it, just return to the truth of God's Word and keep on reminding yourself that it is He who does the work of overcoming. The Bible clearly teaches us that conflicts and struggles will be a part of this life. We will have fears and anxieties because of where we currently live; the earth is infested with sin, and bad things happen here. Along with the fleshly battles we face, we as God's people are engaged in a holy war. Scripture backs this up:

> *For we do not wrestle against flesh and blood, but against principalities, against powers, against the rulers of the darkness of this age, against spiritual* hosts *of wickedness in the heavenly* places.
>
> Ephesians 6:12

I'm becoming more consistent in living as an overcomer. It takes great discipline and practice for me sometimes, especially in regards to my emotions. I know by faith that Jesus has won the battle, whatever my current battle may be. He also reigns as victor of the final battle when all is said and done. So, intellectually I know and I believe. Sometimes, though, my emotions have to be massaged a little to become more spiritually pliable to His tender care.

As a victor, overcomer, and conqueror in Jesus Christ, we will receive hidden manna. We know from the Scriptures we've explored today that our hidden manna is Jesus Christ Himself. One day we will receive Him fully and completely as we stand face to face with the living bread of heaven, and I'm thrilled by the thought of that. But we do not have to wait to receive Him. Jesus is our hidden manna even now.

Feasting on the presence of Jesus strengthens your spirit in the same way that eating fortified energy foods strengthens your body. Let me ask you, sister: are you giving more attention to strengthening your body than you are to strengthening your spirit? Do you delight in feasting on His presence as much as you delight in savoring the richness of food—let's say chocolate or a favorite dessert? I'm not being critical of anyone and her dining persuasions! No, I'm smiling with you right now as we consider these things. Be assured of this: your heavenly Father knows your heart and your desires. He knows mine, too. And He wants to help us desire Him more than anything of this world. He is the living bread that truly satisfies!

Today's Touchpoint

God not only wants us to know His Word, He longs for us to apply it to daily living. I'd like for you to explore ways you can make some life-changing applications today. Some years ago God "smacked" me in the area of my food cravings. When you seriously ask for Him to speak and give you His thoughts on things, He certainly does. His message was this: *Do you want* Me *like you want that food?* I was both amused and convicted in the same moment. I continued asking Him to show me other ways that I was reaching for lesser things to satisfy my desires instead of finding my satisfaction in Him alone.

I challenge you to have a similar conversation with your heavenly Father today. Talk to Him about earthly cravings and heavenly hidden manna, and listen for what He has to say. Enjoy your time together.

Write what you hear God saying below or in your journal.

Dear Jesus, You are the bread of life, and that's enough for me. What a rich banquet it will be feasting on Your presence forever. Thank You, Lord, that You overcame and now invite me to be an overcomer with You. Continue to delight my heart with Your mysteries, Lord. I love You. Amen.

Day 5: Every Day After

Focus: Rising Above the Mundane

Scripture:

"Most assuredly, I say to you, he who hears My word and believes in Him who sent Me has everlasting life, and shall not come into judgment, but has passed from death into life. "

John 5:24

The Lord is my strength and my shield;
my heart trusts in Him, and I am helped.
Therefore my heart rejoices,
and I praise Him with my song.

Psalm 28:7 HCSB

As we've seen throughout the weeks of our study, *Judged, Hurting, Ordinary*, and *Shame* had holy encounters that transformed their lives. All of them faced earthly judgments before meeting Jesus. But as their stories reveal, the only judgment that matters is the judgment of God. And when they met Jesus, they did not encounter condemnation for their sin but mercy and grace and the chance to have true, abundant, everlasting life.

Their stories are our stories. We too have faced the earthly judgments of others. We too have been burdened by sin and shame. But when we met Jesus and gave our hearts and lives to Him, we encountered grace and mercy and crossed over from death into life. Earlier in our study you wrote your testimony of what it was like taking that transforming step. Take a moment now to thank your heavenly Father once again for rescuing you and giving you new life.

We also have something else in common with our four biblical girlfriends, and it is that after our transformational encounter with Jesus, we faced the reality of glory-fading daily living. This is how one woman expressed it:

Sometimes I feel like I'm giving God leftovers instead of first fruits. With the demands and stresses of everyday life, many times I feel like I have nothing left to give Him.

~ Anonymous

This sister nailed it! The demands of life leave you in a tizzy on many days, and day after day of *tizziness* can cause you to become hunkered down in the drudgery of life! This is the very reason I've chosen this theme for the final day of our Bible study. Let me pray for us as we begin our study today:

Dear Father, help us to learn how to rise above the mundane so that even ordinary daily living can be glorious. Amen.

Life can seem particularly mundane after having a mountaintop experience and returning to daily life, can't it? Let's step into the shoes of our sisters from Scripture at the pinnacle of their mountaintop experiences.

Judged was filled with a glorious experience of love as she anointed the feet of Jesus. He sent her away with a blessing, affirming her faith publicly.

How would you have felt in her shoes?

Hurting was healed from twelve years of blood flow. Her faith was affirmed by our Lord as He sent her away to experience restoration and peace.

How would you have felt in her shoes?

Then we have *Ordinary*. During a typical day of coming to the well at noonday in order to miss the tribe of gaggling women, her soul was saturated with the living water.

How would you have felt in her shoes?

Finally, *Shame* made her way to Jesus. It wasn't her initial choice, but she wouldn't have missed it for the world. She was publicly acquitted and cleansed by grace.

How would you have felt in her shoes?

The awareness of this "newness" had to be gloriously pumping through their veins as they stepped away from the Lord. They not only enjoyed the exhilaration that comes from a transformational moment; they sported that get-up-and-go zeal that comes with a fresh new start in life! After their fireworks encounter with Jesus, we part ways with them in Scripture. But we know that each had to return to day-to-day life.

What do you think that life was like for each of these women after the "high place" she experienced when she came face to face with Jesus? Use what you know about each woman from Scripture combined with your imagination to answer the following questions. Remember that your answers will be opinion.

Did *Judged* have difficulty being accepted in her community? Explain.

What kind of issues did *Hurting* encounter after being "unclean" for twelve years?

Did the women of Samaria bring *Ordinary* into their inner circle after she was cleansed by Jesus?

What obstacles did *Shame* encounter after her public humiliation in the Temple courtyard?

The point I'm making here is this: after their dramatic encounters with Jesus, these women had to live out earthly lives that most likely were less than dramatic. Can you relate? Much of life is filled with ordinary, routine living. Does this mean that our spiritual lives must follow suit?

Would you agree or disagree with the following statement?

Although we love the spiritual mountaintop experiences, the truth is that more of our spiritual journey is mundane rather than exciting.

__Agree   __Disagree

If you answered *agree*, I have some really exciting news for you. If you answered *disagree*, then you've already discovered this glorious truth. It's possible to enjoy exhilaration with the Lord each and every day—even in the midst of the routine and ordinary! Though that may sound like a contradiction, stick with me for a moment.

Now, this is a fairly recent revelation for me. I'm not yet proficient in living it out, but I'm certainly getting better at it. That's the whole aim, you know. The longer we walk with Jesus, the more adept we become in taking hold of His glory. Since we spend much of life on the "lower plains" of routine daily living, let's do a little bit of "mind training" to help us stay focused on His glory even after we leave the high places.

Let's take a look at three realities for the believer and how we can counteract each one so that we can live more fulfilling lives with Jesus on a daily basis.

Reality #1: *We tend to crave thrilling spiritual experiences.*

Once you've had a mountaintop experience with the Lord, you want more! Your heart longs to stay there, enjoying Him and sensing His presence. As the emotions fade and you slink down that mountainside into the plains, oh how you miss the exhilaration of it all.

Describe a time when you were coming off a mountaintop experience. How did you feel as you returned to ordinary life?

My friend, it takes the grace of Almighty God to keep you encouraged in your devotion to Him in the ordinariness of life, especially in those times when you don't *feel* Him. It also takes much more discipline to pray and read His Word during these times.

Counterattack: *Journal your feelings to God.*

Tell God how thankful you are that He is there even in the ordinariness of life, even when you don't feel His presence. Ask your helper the Holy Spirit to affirm God's love and presence in your life. Let your journaling be accompanied by worship. One of the greatest ways I've discovered to come out of the spiritual blues is to sit down with my hymnal and sing the great old hymns. Many of the hymnwriters of old were theologians, so you'll find powerful lyrics straight from the Bible. Contemporary praise and worship songs can achieve the same results. Praise lifts our spiritual eyes upward and refocuses us on God.

Reality #2: *Life is busy, making it difficult to find time to have devotional moments with God.*

Years ago I was writing material to help women sort out time management issues. Of course, I sought God's guidance on this topic because I truly understand the time constraints brought on by the busyness of life. Like the contemporary anonymous woman at the beginning of today's lesson, we often feel like we're giving Him leftovers instead of coming to Him with our first fruits. As I sought God's take on time management, He dropped a verse right into my mind.

Counterattack: *Read and meditate on Malachi 3:10.*

This is the verse God dropped into my mind. I remember laughing, telling Him that it was an unusual verse to help with time management because it is about tithing, not time. But in just a moment it made sense to me as I realized it relates to blessings regarding obedience, consistency, and first fruits. God revealed to me how this verse is pertinent to my daily devotional time with Him. You see, He rushes to bless our obedience to love Him when we give Him our busy schedule. Just as He honors our gifts of money, so He honors our gifts of time.

Take a look for yourself at Malachi 3:10 on the following page, and see what God reveals to you. Spend some time talking to God about how this verse relates to spending time with Him. Write your thoughts below.

*"Bring all the tithes into the storehouse, / That there may be food in My house, / And try Me now in this," / Says the L*ORD *of hosts, / "If I will not open for you the windows of heaven / And pour out for you such blessing / That there will not be room enough to receive it." (Malachi 3:10)*

Reality #3: *It can be extremely difficult to stay focused during quiet time with the Lord.*

From what I hear from women, this concern is right up there with the concern about having no time. In fact, it intrigues me that so many women say they can't stay focused and think they are the only ones experiencing this. Remember, the enemy of God will do everything he can to keep you distracted and discouraged when you try to have a quiet time with the Lord. Knowing that should help you be more determined than ever to have one!

Counterattack: *Choose some ways that you can be single focused in other areas of your life, and put them into practice.*

I began this particular counterattack a couple of years ago, and it has been very effective in helping me to be more focused during my devotion time. It occurred to me—and I'm sure it was an insight from the Holy Spirit—that a reason I couldn't stay focused during my time with Jesus was that I was not practicing being focused in other areas of my life.

For example, think of focusing solely on your food while eating instead of being distracted with the phone, computer, and so forth. Or drive in silence, concentrating on your surroundings, rather than driving with the radio on and letting your mind wander.

List two or three areas where you will determine to practice the art of staying focused. After a week or so, record your improvement in your journal.

These counterattacks are designed to provide simplicity, consistency, and focus to your daily worship and quiet time experience. They are so simple and basic that you may be tempted to dismiss them. But I encourage you to try them. Although we can certainly seek God through high technology and sophisticated methods, His call to simplicity and an easy-flowing spirit connects with my heart. Even in the ordinary and often tedious or complex tasks of daily life, we can experience pervading peace and joy when we approach all that we do with a reverent attitude of worship, keeping our focus on Jesus. I encourage you to answer God's call to focused simplicity in your love relationship with Him.

I believe a focus on Jesus is likely what sustained our four anonymous sisters from Scripture. Though we do not know what happened to them after their encounters with Jesus, I believe we know enough from Scripture to know that they were changed—transformed. It follows that the challenges and mundane tasks these women faced "after Jesus" must have been somehow different than before because *they* were different "after Jesus." They each had a brand new identity.

I believe that what happened on the inside of each of them gloriously transformed her outward appearance. Jesus does that, you know. You cannot be gloriously changed in your soul without the radiance of Jesus shining through to others.

When Jesus enters our life, we are never the same. As we grow in our love for Him by getting to know Him through His Word, the world notices. Some of the most striking examples of God's glory are shining through those who are traveling through suffering and heartache. We also see God's glory illuminated in lives that, humanly speaking, are rather ordinary. Yet they have discovered that because of Jesus, every day can be glorious! It's not about our circumstances but our glorious Lord living on the inside of us!

We, like our four anonymous sisters, have new life within us. Because of this reality, we have every reason to rejoice! Oh, my friend, take just a moment and celebrate the fact that you have passed from death into life. Stop for just a moment and take joy in the fact that the Lord, who loves you beyond comprehension, is your strength and shield. You've been changed on the inside! Now, let the world know!

Today's Touchpoint

Well, my friend, it's time to lay this study aside. But please don't place it too far away. My prayer is that you'll revisit these truths from God's Word and the things that He spoke specifically to you throughout our time together.

In conclusion, how about sharing in a few words about your greatest take-away from our six weeks of study?

My greatest take-away:

One day we'll enjoy a grand reunion with our new girlfriends *Judged, Hurting, Ordinary,* and *Shame,* only we won't use those names for we will know their real ones! Even better, we will have the thrill of knowing that both they and we will have new names as well! I can almost see us now—you, me, and them, sitting and chattering while we caress our dazzling white stones.

Until then, take hold of God's hand and connect with His heart for your journey ahead. He loves you and knows you by name, *right now.* You are His special somebody—for this moment and every moment hereafter!

Join me in a final prayer together:

Dear heavenly Father, words can't express my thankfulness for Your glory that sustains us in this journey of life. Thank You for all that You have taught us. Thank You for showing us that we have a special place in Your heart. Father, bless my new sisters who have joined together through this Bible study. I ask that You refresh and strengthen us. Fill us with excitement in the walk You've prepared specifically for each one of us. May we recall our journey together often during the days ahead. But more than that, may we recall You and Your personal faithfulness to us. In the matchless Name above all names, Jesus, I pray. Amen.

Week 6
Video Viewer Guide

• • • • • • • • • • • • • • • • • • • •

And from the throne proceeded lightnings, thunderings, and voices. Seven lamps of fire were burning before the throne, which are the seven Spirits of God.

Revelation 4:5 NKJV

"God is Spirit, and those who worship Him must worship in spirit and truth."

John 4:24 NKJV

Let God do a work in your life:

Grow in your _____.

Grow in your _____,

helping you to grasp who He really is and who you really are in Him.

Are you tired? Worn out? Burned out on religion? Come to me. Get away with me and you'll recover your life. I'll show you how to take a real rest. Walk with me and work with me—watch how I do it. Learn the unforced rhythms of grace. I won't lay anything heavy or ill-fitting on you. Keep company with me and you'll learn how to live freely and lively.

Matthew 11:28-30 *The Message*

Do you need a fresh start? . . . I know where you can get it. In the very

_____ of God.

To [she] who overcomes I will give some of the hidden manna to eat. And

I will give [her] a white _____, and on the stone a new

_____ written which no one knows except [her].

Revelation 2:17 NKJV

Notes

Week 2

1. Cindi Wood, *I've Used All My Sick Days, Now I'll Have to Call in Dead* (Nashville: Creative Dimensions, 1988), iii.
2. *hamartōlos*, http://www.blueletterbible.org/lang/lexicon/lexicon.cfm?Strongs=G268&t=KJV.
3. *judgment*, http://www.thefreedictionary.com/judgment.
4. *eiréné*, http://biblehub.com/greek/1515.htm.

Week 3

1. *kathab*, http://bibleapps.com/hebrew/3789.htm.
2. *juncture*, http://www.merriam-webster.com/dictionary/juncture.
3. *thlipsis*, http://www.blueletterbible.org/lang/lexicon/lexicon.cfm?Strongs=G2347.
4. *pistis*, http://studybible.info/strongs/G4102.
5. *sōzō*, http://studybible.info/search/KJV/G4982.
6. *eiréné*, http://biblehub.com/greek/1515.htm.

Week 4

1. *dei*, http://www.blueletterbible.org/lang/lexicon/lexicon.cfm?Strongs=G1163.
2. *kopiao*, http://www.biblestudytools.com/lexicons/greek/kjv/kopiao.html.
3. *Matthew Henry's Complete Commentary on the Whole Bible Vol. V, Christian Classics Ethereal Library*, http://www.ccel.org/ccel/henry/mhc5.John.v.html.
4. *hallomai*, http://www.biblestudytools.com/lexicons/greek/nas/hallomai.html.

Week 5

1. Cindi Wood, *Desperate: Seeking Simplicity, Finding the Cross* (Nashville: LifeWay, 2012) 88.
2. "Power in the Blood," Lewis E. Jones, 1899, http://www.hymnary.org/text/would_you_be_free_from_the_burden_jones.
3. *hamartanō*, http://www.blueletterbible.org/lang/lexicon/lexicon.cfm?Strongs=G264.
4. *pesha`*, http://www.blueletterbible.org/lang/lexicon/lexicon.cfm?strongs=H6588.
5. *katēgoros*, http://www.blueletterbible.org/lang/lexicon/lexicon.cfm?Strongs=G2725.

Week 6

1. Definition of *"given name,"* http://dictionary.reference.com/browse/given+name.
2. http://www.biblestudytools.com/commentaries/revelation/revelation-2/revelation-2-17.html.
3. *psephos*, http://www.blueletterbible.org/lang/lexicon/lexicon.cfm?strongs=g5586&t=kjv.
4. *leukos*, http://www.blueletterbible.org/lang/lexicon/lexicon.cfm?Strongs=G3022.
5. *Ebenezer*, 1 Samuel 7:12, http://www.biblegateway.com/passage/?search=1+Samuel+7%3A12 & version=NKJV.